Trends in Comparative Law and Economics

Nuno Garoupa

T0352113

ANTHEM PRESS

Anthem Press
An imprint of Wimbledon Publishing Company
www.anthempress.com

This edition first published in UK and USA 2024
by ANTHEM PRESS
75–76 Blackfriars Road, London SE1 8HA, UK
or PO Box 9779, London SW19 7ZG, UK
and
244 Madison Ave #116, New York, NY 10016, USA

First published in the UK and USA by Anthem Press in 2022

Copyright © Nuno Garoupa 2024

The author asserts the moral right to be identified as the author of this work.

All rights reserved. Without limiting the rights under copyright reserved above,
no part of this publication may be reproduced, stored or introduced into
a retrieval system, or transmitted, in any form or by any means
(electronic, mechanical, photocopying, recording or otherwise),
without the prior written permission of both the copyright
owner and the above publisher of this book.

British Library Cataloguing-in-Publication Data
A catalogue record for this book is available from the British Library.

Library of Congress Control Number: 2024932432

ISBN-13: 978-1-83999-192-9 (Pbk)
ISBN-10: 1-83999-192-5 (Pbk)

This title is also available as an e-book.

CONTENTS

To my two beloved daughters, Beatriz and Anna:
there is no life worth living without knowledge!

Chapter 1

INTRODUCTION

Comparative law and economics is a growing area of interest in the interaction between law and economics, comparative law, comparative economics and comparative political science. It includes both strands of the more traditional literature, namely the role of legal families from comparative law, and the microeconomic analysis of legal rules from conventional law and economics.

Whether teaching a short seminar on comparative law and economics or including a few sessions on the subject in a semester-long course on comparative law, difficulties arise when one searches for a bibliography—this is true whether one is preparing a mandatory or suggested reading list for students. It is always a struggle to find a comprehensive and appropriate comparative law and economics reference list.

One possible way to introduce the subject to students is to assemble a collection of seminal articles on appropriate topics. There are a few difficulties in introducing students to the subject in this way. First, due to the multidisciplinary nature of comparative law and economics, the language is often inconsistent across articles. Second, some articles are difficult for an audience not very familiar with formal mathematical models or advanced econometrics. Third, in subject matter, there is a widespread lack of harmony; there is even a lack of consistency in the acknowledgment of different authors, topics and approaches in comparative law and economics.

The alternative approach is to look for a more comprehensive source that systematically provides an approachable overview of comparative law and economics. Mattei (1998) is still an excellent seminal reference, but this book largely predates the rise and dominance of the legal origins' theory in the debate between and among scholars, policymakers and international organizations such as the World Bank. More recent readings include De Geest (2009) and Eisenberg and Ramello (2016). Both books present a wonderful collection of insightful and noteworthy articles in comparative law and economics, but they are neither organized nor intended as a short introduction to students and researchers. They do not serve as a comprehensive roadmap to a more provocative and ambitious syllabus.

There are useful methodological overviews such as the ones provided by Caterina (2012) and Faust (2019). As a leading scholar in law and economics, Ogus offers plenty of comparative law examples in his excellent and engaging paperback (Ogus 2006). Another leading scholar in the field includes references to comparative law and economics in a more general introduction to comparative law (De Geest 2020). However, these materials are too succinct to satisfy the curious student, the dedicated scholar or the motivated reader.

The current book can be seen as a comprehensive introduction, a helpful guide to additional reading in either comparative law or law and economics and a primer textbook for a short course or seminar in comparative law and economics. It should be understood as a quick reference in comparative law and economics as the field stands in recent times.

The present book opens with a short introduction about methods in general in Chapter 2. It also reviews recent developments, namely empirical legal studies and behavioral law and economics.

The standard discussion between common-law and civil-law legal families follows.[1] In Chapter 3, different institutions and mechanisms that play an important role in the economic analysis of legal systems are considered. This chapter reflects scholarship largely independent of the remarkable and influential legal origins' theory. Chapter 4 brings the reader to the debate, to use the [famous] words of Michaels (2009), about the first wave of comparative law and economics—the famous legal origins' theory.

A large part of comparative law and economics is about applying microeconomic analysis of legal rules to assess differences and similarities, particularly from an efficiency standpoint. Chapter 5 provides for a general overview of private law and economics. For each relevant topic, the chapter includes a summary of the overall framework (particularly useful for those readers with less familiarity with conventional law and economics) followed by a comparative law application (bona fide purchase and titling in property law and economics; the principle of *non-cumul* in the interaction of contract and tort law and economics; the Good Samaritan principle in tort law and economics; and cost-shifting rules and judicial interest rate in the economics of civil procedure). Chapter 6 proposes a comprehensive view of comparative administrative law and economics to develop a more unified outlook of a growing area.

---

1 One will use "common-law" to refer to the legal family and "common law" to refer to the particular rules and practices of the English or American legal systems.

Comparative judicial politics is usually not regarded as part of comparative law and economics. However, the comparative study of judicial behavior and courts cannot be ignored by those interested in understanding comparative law from an economic perspective. Therefore, Chapter 7 suggests a list of important insights in models of judicial behavior, dissent theory and strategic defection theory.

If judges matter, so do lawyers. Lawyering is covered by Chapter 8, with an emphasis on economic explanations for varying regulations of the legal profession around the world. The book concludes with a short summary of possible research developments and challenges to comparative law and economics.

The book aims for a large audience across both law and economics (and possibly wider afield such as political science or development studies). Therefore, all chapters are written in a nontechnical language (avoiding statistics, mathematical formulas, formal models, regression tables, etc.). In particular, the book assumes little previous knowledge of traditional law and economics, thus making the more economic-oriented contents accessible to legal scholars outside of conventional comparative law and economics (e.g., those interested in law and development, law and society or empirical legal studies).

To facilitate reading, there is a limited use of citations and references. Nevertheless, many debates covered in this primer might require more advanced reading for those looking for a deeper understanding of the arguments and disagreements among scholars. Therefore, each chapter builds on previous work that is appropriately cited and, consequently, always available to the reader looking for sources, ideas and more advanced exposition of scholarship.

In a short introduction like this one, many other important topics and subjects have been left out. Some were excluded because they require a textbook on their own, such as the role of rational choice theory in comparative constitutional law. Others have been excluded because they are still too embryonic, such as comparative family law or economics and comparative criminal law and economics. All options reflect my own understanding of the field and are inevitably subject to dispute.

This book is only possible because I have been lucky to work with many talented scholars to whom I am deeply grateful—in particular, Sofia Amaral-Garcia, Carlos Gómez-Ligüerre, Laarni Escresa, Tom Ginsburg, Peter Grajzl, Milan Markovic, Lela Melón, Mariana Pargendler and Tom Ulen. Many chapters of this book are based on previous articles and research projects that would have been impossible without their collaboration, assistance and guidance. I am also grateful to all my other coauthors who are not directly cited in the book—unfortunately, they are too many to be named here.

My sincere gratitude goes to each and every single one of them for their coauthorships, efforts and contributions. The same appreciation extends to my colleagues at the four wonderful institutions where I taught comparative law and economics in the United States (University of Illinois College of Law, University of Alabama School of Law, Texas A&M University School of Law and George Mason University Antonin Scalia Law School). I have benefited from many useful comments and insightful critiques at many conferences, seminars, workshops and colloquia around the world where the original sources for this book were presented. I cannot forget the members of the former Comparative Law and Economics Forum (CLEF) who embraced me in 2001 and offered an amazing venue for discussion for almost two decades.[2] Finally, a word of sincere gratitude to all my students at the different courses and seminars where I have covered comparative law and economics. Outside of the United States, I should mention the law schools of Católica Global Law School in Portugal, University of Manchester in the UK, Universitat Pompeu Fabra in Spain, Bucerius Law School in Germany, University of Hamburg in Germany, Tel Aviv University Buchmann Faculty of Law in Israel, Amsterdam Centre for Law and Economics in the Netherlands, Fundação Getúlio Vargas—Rio de Janeiro in Brazil and Universidad de Bahía Blanca in Argentina. This book would have been more difficult to structure and produce without their extremely generous feedback. Karyn R. Christensen provided excellent research assistance in the final stages of production of this primer.

---

2 See Garoupa and Ulen (2021) for a summary of CLEF activities and goals.

Chapter 2

COMPARATIVE LAW AND ECONOMICS[1]

Comparative law and economics fuses two distinct terms: "comparative law" and "law and economics." Before we settle on the conceptual meaning of "comparative law and economics," it is important to explore these two terms separately.

a) Law and economics

By "law and economics," one is referring to the field of study that uses the tools of microeconomics to study the law. For example, consider negligence liability in the context of tort law: there has been an accident, a victim has been injured and an injurer has been identified. Under tort law, a court ought to find the injurer liable for money damages to compensate the victim if that injurer failed to take "reasonable care." If the injurer did take reasonable care or if the victim failed to take her own reasonable care, then the injurer ought not to be liable. The economic view of negligence provides a more precise view of what care should count as "reasonable." According to law and economics, the social costs of accidents will be minimized if actors invest in "cost-justified precaution." "Cost-justified precaution" is a precaution in which the cost is less than the expected accident losses; this precaution prevents an accident or mitigates losses.

To further illustrate, suppose that there has been an accident involving two motorists. One of whom is clearly the injurer; the other, the victim, has suffered losses (such as damage to her car, medical expenses for her own injuries and lost income from an inability to work). The injurer will be held liable to the victim for her damages if the precaution that would have prevented the accident (such as not speeding or obeying the traffic rules) cost less than the probability that the accident would have occurred times the

---

1 Extensive parts of this chapter follow from Garoupa and Ginsburg (2012) and Garoupa and Ulen (2021).

victim's losses, and the injurer did not take that precaution. If he did take the precaution but an accident happened anyway, he will be (or should be) excused from negligence liability for the victim's losses. The victim will have to bear her own losses.

Where a more traditional legal analysis narrows in on what should happen if there is litigation, as in the example above, law and economics focuses on how law can influence preaccident behavior so that accidents are far less likely to happen or are less injurious if they do occur. That is, law and economics imagines that if potential injurers know (perhaps through their lawyers) the actions that will excuse them from negligence liability in the event of an accident, then they will take adequate precaution—that is, precaution whose cost is less than the expected benefit to a potential victim.

There are, of course, important details that one has either touched on lightly or skipped over. What role should contributory negligence play? What is comparative negligence's role? When should strict liability be the standard and when, negligence liability? How should the tort liability system and the *ex ante* safety regulation system collaborate (whether by statute or administrative agency)—should they act as complements or substitutes? These and other important questions can be approached with the tools of economics.

Take a second example. Consider the probability and severity of punishment. Individuals consider the personal benefit of violating the law (such as gratification or financial gains) as well as the possibility of punishment. However, punishment is intrinsically probabilistic since law enforcement agencies do not have infinite resources to monitor every single action by every single individual. If probability and severity of punishment are not sufficiently persuasive, individuals are undeterred and do not comply with the law. An economic view of crime and punishment considers optimal law enforcement. In other words, an economic view seeks to find the appropriate combination of punishment probability and severity to deter individuals. The reason this quest is important is because law enforcement is costly; one wants to find the optimal balance between costs imposed on society by criminal actions and by financing law enforcement.

When different types of punishment are considered, whether it be monetary fines, imprisonment or other formal and informal sanctions, multiple complications arise in terms of social costs. Moreover, since punishment is probabilistic, individual risk preferences are expected to play an important role. Individuals who dislike risk may respond to the probabilistic punishment in different ways than individuals who seek risk. Finally, violating the law can take different forms and consequences, depending on specific contexts. For example, speeding and murdering are two actions that violate the law, yet they are very distinct in their nature and moral invalidation. The tools of economics can provide some answers to these multiple considerations.

A final example of traditional law and economics is legal costs in litigation. When contemplating filing a lawsuit, a plaintiff must assess (1) the possible gain, including the probability of winning and the potential award (not necessarily limited to a monetary amount), and (2) litigation costs. One expects a lawsuit when the possible gains offset litigation costs. An economic question is if allocating litigation costs to the losing party (a so-called cost-shifting rule) increases or decreases litigation rates. The answer depends on how cost-shifting rules impact actual litigation costs and the probability of winning (including the potential award). This analysis differentiates between exogenous (mere reallocation of fixed litigation costs across plaintiff and defendant) and endogenous (variable litigation costs respond to reallocation rules) economic reasonings.

From all these illustrations, one can say that law and economics explores the answer to two fundamental questions: (a) a positive question concerning the impact of laws and regulations on the behavior of individuals, in terms of their decisions and the implications for social welfare; and (b) a normative question concerning the relative advantages of laws in terms of efficiency and social welfare. To answer these two questions, law and economics applies the methodology of microeconomic analysis. Microeconomic analysis makes certain simplifying assumptions; individuals respond to incentives and make their decisions in a rational way, comparing costs and benefits, given all the available information. More recent developments have relaxed the assumption of full rationality to adopt a more realistic limited rationality assumption in the context of the "behavioral law and economics." Another assumption is that the welfare of society is measured by aggregating the individual welfare of its members, although this could raise some methodological objections (such as the inclusion of illegal gains in social welfare maximization).

Today, law and economics is one of the most influential scholarly methodologies in American legal thinking. The origins of the field can be traced back to the eighteenth and nineteenth centuries, for example, with the writings of Bentham (1789). Law and economics gained notoriety with the articles of Nobel laureates Ronald Coase (1960) and Gary Becker (1968) and the books of Guido Calabresi (1970) and Richard Posner (1972). In the last sixty years, law and economics has expanded to all areas of the law. This expansion started with those with more obvious economic significance (antitrust and regulation, tax, corporate governance, bankruptcy, employment) to the hard core of legal studies (contracts, tort, property, crime, civil and criminal procedure) and new areas of the law (family law, environmental law and constitutional law and institutions).[2]

b) Empirical legal studies

An important recent development in law and economics is the rise of empirical legal studies.[3] Using experiments, data from public archives, case data, and more, law and economics scholars, among others, have subjected hypotheses about legal issues to data to see whether the real world agrees with or refutes those hypotheses. To take one famous example, John Donohue and Steve Levitt argued in a 2001 study that half of the remarkable decline in crime that began in the United States in 1991 can be attributed causally to the legalization of abortion by the U.S. Supreme Court in *Roe v. Wade* in 1973. Since their controversial study, the number of empirical studies explaining crime rate trends since the 1970s in the United States has exploded.

A different illustration comes from empirical studies in comparative judicial politics. Initially almost limited to the U.S. Supreme Court, empirical studies have now extended to almost every supreme and constitutional court around the world. For example, the myth that judges in civil-law jurisdictions are insulated from politics has now been fully discredited by solid empirical evidence.[4]

More recently, data collection and availability has helped scholars test the common-law/civil-law distinction against substance of the law. As an example, Bradford and her coauthors show in their 2021 article that, while the common-law/civil-law distinction seems somehow persuasive in property law, it is unreliable when it comes to assess antitrust law. Therefore, empirical studies suggest that legal families may not reflect legal substance in relevant areas of the law as previously assumed by some influential economists.

c) Behavioral law and economics

"Behavioral law and economics" is another area that has recently developed.[5] Behavioral science (or behavioral economics) imports the findings of cognitive and social psychology into legal decisions and economic choices. The importance of this innovation is that it supplements the sophisticated and

---

2 See Cooter and Ulen (2016) and Shavell (2004) for excellent introductions to the field. For more advanced reading, consider Parisi (2017).

3 See Lawless et al. (2016) for an excellent introduction to the field.

4 See Garoupa et al. (2021) for an extensive overview of the literature.

5 See Zamir and Teichman (2018) for an excellent introduction to the field.

unrealistic view of decision making (called "rational choice theory"), which has long been the prevailing theory in microeconomics, with a more realistic view of fallible human decisions.

Rational choice theory assumes that individuals are rational in the sense that their preferences are complete (if any given goods or services are A and B, an individual can prefer A to B, B to A or be indifferent between A and B) and transitive (if A is preferred to B and B is preferred to C, then A is necessarily preferred to C). Therefore, rational individuals' actions are well suited to achieving their goals. An implication of the standard rational choice theory is that rational people do not make mistakes unless they are misled or misinformed.

Behavioral economics does not claim that humans are irrational. It holds, rather, that humans make predictable mistakes when making individual choices. Those mistakes have been established by careful experimentation. In addition, behavioral economists and psychologists have attempted to discern the methods by which decision making can be "debiased" from these mistakes.

For example, standard microeconomics proposes that individuals have attitudes toward risk that influence people's decisions when faced with uncertainty: people are either risk-averse, risk-neutral or risk-seeking. Those categories speak for themselves. It is important to note that standard microeconomics imagines that if a person is risk-averse, they are risk-averse with respect to any decision about an uncertain course of action. It does not matter, for example, whether the uncertainty arises from a gain (as in buying a winning lottery ticket) or a loss (as in a house fire). However, as has been shown in multiple experiments and scientific articles, most people are risk-averse with respect to gains but risk-seeking with respect to losses. Due to this finding, people's choices can be affected—indeed, changed—by how a choice is framed—that is, how the choices are presented. For instance, if people are presented with a choice between public health options, both of which frame the choice by focusing on lives saved, they behave in a risk-averse manner. However, if people are presented with precisely the same choice between public health options that frame the choice by focusing on lives lost, then people behave in a risk-seeking manner.

d) Comparative economics

Before the fall of the Soviet Union in the early 1990s, an important field in economics was comparative economic systems. It studied differences between capitalism and socialism (and fascism, but in much less extent after WWII) in terms of major macroeconomic variables (such as GDP growth rates), allocation of resources (consumption and production patterns) and other socially relevant indicators (such as inequality or unemployment). There was some tradition of institutional analysis, broadly speaking, but the analysis was not really focused on law or legal institutions in the way of modern law and economics. Scholars concentrated on the different economic merits of each system (capitalism, socialism and variations in between, such as market socialism or Yugoslav self-management) in promoting growth and effective public policy. These scholars recognized the role played by institutions. However, law and legal institutions (e.g., property and contracts) were usually bundled with political and social institutions in some simplified framework. There was never, for example, such a field as Soviet law and economics.

With the fall of communism and the transition from socialism to market-oriented economies, a new form of comparative economics developed. It came to be known as "transition economics." Scholars studied central and east European countries as they implemented their economic reforms and then later, China and Vietnam. A debate emerged that was largely about gradualism versus shock therapy in economic reforms. Institutions played a crucial role, specifically in the debate over privatization in former socialist Europe. Yet law was somehow neglected, with a few important exceptions. It could be argued that the lack of more serious attention to law and legal institutions somehow undermined the economic understanding of transitions.

By the early 2000s, transition economics faded into development economics. Meanwhile, a new comparative economics emerged, focused on civil-law versus common-law legal families. Based on the legal origins' theory (see Chapter 4), the relationship between civil-law and common-law is explored in a reasoning logically similar to the relationship between socialism/centrally planned economies and capitalism/market economies. The underlying argument is that institutions are designed to minimize both private and state expropriations. Common-law legal institutions are inclined to mitigate state power (as markets are) while civil-law legal institutions are focused on eliminating private disordering (as central planning is). Within this framework, the importance of legal institutions is, at least, as important as political, social and economic institutions. However, the unbundling of institutions, particularly between the legal and the political, has been subject to a significant debate.

e) Comparative law

Comparative law can be understood as a method, for example, the methodology of comparing laws and legal institutions across jurisdictions, including the so-called functionalist approach. Still, comparative law can also be recognized as an object, namely the description of similarities and differences between the laws and legal institutions of different countries.[6]

The relationship between comparative law and law and economics can be described in one word: uneasy. Part of the difficulty is methodological. Law and economics focuses on analysis, particularly on causal analysis. The scholarly goal of law and economics is a demonstration that a particular legal rule or standard is efficient. Clearly, that demonstration can be made theoretically or empirically or both.

In comparative law, the first order of business is an accurate description of the legal rules in the jurisdictions to be compared. This description is frequently an excruciatingly complex affair. Contract rules in X and Z may both appear to deal with, say, punitive amounts of damages for breach. But do they really? Perhaps one is just supra-compensatory damages for idiosyncratic losses, while the other is purely punitive. And whatever the differences may be on the books, how are they really treated in practice? A comparatist may spend the bulk of her scholarly energy making certain that the legal rules being compared are truly identical.

One specific concern in mind is the interaction between law and economics and functionalist comparative law. Efficiency could be a/the "functionalist standard" for purposes of legal analysis, but comparative law scholars tend to dislike it. Therefore, for the purpose of the term "comparative law and economics," it is easier if one understands "comparative law" to be the object while "law and economics" to be the method. Under "comparative law" as the object and "law and economics" as the method, one can realize that comparative law is potentially in an excellent position to help law and economics by providing two wonderful tools. First, comparative law provides for a serious effort into tracking legal change (e.g., new developments in negligence rules or contract practices around the world) that can motivate economic puzzles (such as the impact of changed or redesigned incentives). Second, comparative law is rich in relevant historical examples to support or undermine economic modeling efforts. However, the communication between comparative law and law and economics requires addressing additional challenges before it can be presented as simply "comparative law and economics." From the viewpoint of comparative law, the focus on institutionally detailed complexity and the option for a multiplicity of normative goals that shape comparative law analysis must be reexamined. From the perspective of law

---

6 See Siems (2018) for an excellent introduction to the field. For more advanced reading, consider Reimann and Zimmermann (2019).

and economics, one must recognize the need to simplify the formal modeling or econometrics for analytical trackability and, at the same time, relax the focus on efficiency.

f) Comparative law and economics: Is it a field of study?

In the narrowest sense, as one has seen, comparative law and economics is the application of the methodology of law and economics to study comparative law. Still, such notion has faced several challenges. First, before the rise of the legal origins' theory, standard applications of law and economics to specific topics in comparative private or public law did not generate extensive attention by law and economics specialists or comparative law scholars.[7]

Second, the legal origins' theory itself has not been promoted or induced by legal economists working in the traditions of law and economics, but rather by development and financial economists. This first wave of comparative law and economics received a cold reaction by comparative law scholars. They found it oversimplistic, dubious (based on the excessive belief of common-law as private market outcomes and civil-law as state-desired outcomes) and unconvincing (according to comparative law scholars, the direct causal link between law, economic growth and social engineering is undertheorized, probably indirect and tenuous). It also provoked mixed reactions by legal economists. While the empirical evidence generated an extensive literature, the earlier version of the legal origins' theory ignored many other relevant mechanisms such as transplants, legal culture and endogenous innovation. Furthermore, the role of path dependence ignored the realities of globalization and profound legal change. Although based on a general principle that convergence of legal systems could be studied as a movement toward efficiency, the legal origins' theory imposed the view that divergence inevitably means inefficiency. Many law and economics scholars did not share an enthusiasm for a theory that suggests that "one size fits all."

A new wave of comparative law and economics has emerged in the last decade, beyond the common-law/civil-law distinction, with a focus on the role of legal culture and quality of law in context (including enforcement).[8] In this respect, this second wave of comparative law and economics is broader and with a greater focus on the role of legal framework within comparative economics.

---

7 An important exception is Mattei (1998).

8 One follows Michaels (2009) in making a distinction between legal origins' theory as first wave and recent developments as second wave of comparative law and economics.

Comparative law and economics has benefited from both empirical legal studies and behavioral law and economics. Traditionally, empirical comparative law and economics has been significantly constrained by the availability of comparable data across multiple jurisdictions. Still, the methodology is there: in ranking law and legal institutions (ultimately, based on law and economics notions of efficiency), producing general hypotheses and testing these hypotheses (not within specific jurisdictions as in the more conventional approach, but rather by cross-country regressions).[9] Behavioral comparative law and economics is a promising innovation by highlighting different underlying cultural preferences.[10]

9 Ramello provides an excellent summary in his introduction to Eisenberg and Ramello (2016).
10 Caterina (2012) suggests an interesting application, for example, in the use and interpretation of the popular ultimatum game from a comparative perspective.

Chapter 3

LAW AND ECONOMICS
OF LEGAL FAMILIES[1]

The relationship between comparative law literature and economic scholarship on legal families is replete with remarkable ironies. The legal origins' theory, as one will see in the following chapter, relies heavily on the classifications of legal families devised by comparative law scholars. Yet economists popularized the concept of legal families precisely when comparative lawyers began to abandon this landmark contribution of their own field.

a) Common-law and civil-law

Comparisons among foreign legal systems, whether casual or profound, have a long history—and so does the idea that English law is significantly different from the French and Roman law. The effort to extrapolate from differing legal systems and divide the world map into a handful of "legal families" based on the heritage and character of the underlying legal systems is far more recent. This approach is closely intertwined with the history of modern-day comparative law itself, a discipline whose birth, for most scholars, dates to about the early 1900s. However, reigning conceptions of legal families have varied over time, casting doubt on the systematic reliability and historicity of these categories.

The central importance of legal families as one of the main theoretical achievements of comparative law came in the 1960s due to the work of important comparative law scholars, including Konrad Zweigert and Hein Kötz. In 1969, these authors proposed a well-known classificatory, recognizing common-law and civil-law systems. They subdivided the civil-law family into three separate branches: the French, the German and the

---

1 Extensive parts of this chapter follow from Garoupa (2018), Garoupa and Ginsburg (2012), Garoupa and Pargendler (2014) and Garoupa and Ulen (2021).

Scandinavian civil-law systems. The three civil-law families, together with the common-law, far-Eastern law, Islamic law and Hindu law families, defined the main "styles" of legal systems around the globe. The scheme advanced by Zweigert and Kötz was widely popular and came to be the substantial basis for the literature on legal families. This categorization was, remarkably, of relatively minor importance in their treatise, whose primary purpose was to redefine the study of comparative law in functional terms. This intellectual ambition was far different from the legal families' project.

The rapidly expanding legal origins' theory (see Chapter 4) in the late 1990s related conventional legal-family classifications to major economic variables and relevant puzzles in the development literature (e.g., why some countries grow successfully and others do not, why there is a trap for middle-income countries, which legal institutions are important in explaining successful and unsuccessful reforms). At the same time, significant developments in the finance literature occurred (in this case, under the original name of "law and finance"). Significant developments included empirical studies employing legal families to explain cross-country variation in issues as diverse labor markets regulation, entry restrictions, government ownership of banks and the media and military conscription.

Economic literature has investigated the hypothesis that the common-law system is particularly conducive to economic growth in opposition to civil-law, in particular French law. This is an essentially empirical vein of scholarship. It defends the notion that legal systems originated in the English common-law have superior institutions for economic growth and development than those of French civil-law. According to the proponents of this empirical view, there are essentially two reasons for the link between the common-law and economic growth. First, common-law provides more adequate institutions for financial markets and business transactions generally, and that in turn fuels economic growth. These institutions might include more efficient substantive rules, as well as mechanisms by which the common-law tends to develop such rules. Second, civil-law presupposes a greater role for state intervention that is detrimental for economic freedom and market efficiency. The relationship between growth or economic performance and legal system carries an implicit assumption—law and legal institutions matter for economic growth. This has been a staple of institutional economics for decades, since Douglas North (1990), but nevertheless, debatable.

The alleged pro-market bias of the common-law (the idea of some Hayekian bottom-up efficiencies in the English legal system as opposed to some top-down inefficiencies in the French legal system) is an important argument. However, the existence of some antimarket bias in French law is intrinsically debatable. Even the thesis that French law is less effective than the common-law in protecting property rights from state predation has been disputed by economists. In fact, as discussed in Chapter 4, the current models developed to explain these differences have been subject to serious criticism.

Stability of the law is a conventional argument to favor judge-made law with deference to precedent against systematic and chaotic legislative production. However, empirically it is not clear that case law is more stable than legislation. In addition, the argument that the common-law is more stable undercuts other claims that the mechanism for its efficiency lies in the selection of disputes for litigation.

Another possible channel by which the common-law might support growth is the enhanced willingness in common-law jurisdictions to allow choice of law. But globalization of business transactions has exerted enormous pressure for change in civil-law jurisdictions in this respect. Overall, it might well be that the common-law is more efficient and positively correlated with economic growth, but the causation remains undertheorized to a larger extent as one notices in Chapter 4. The mechanism for the efficiency of the common-law versus (French) civil-law is intrinsically convoluted and debatable.

b) Convergence of legal systems

If legal families are based on history and tradition, a straightforward question asks the extent to which they have changed and converged in the last decades with globalization, other technology and economic developments. Comparative law scholars are divided about the answer. Legal economists have entered the debate about the convergence of legal systems and the role of harmonization. One explanation legal economists have offered is that, when there is freedom of choice as to the legal regime to be used, competition between legal systems should emerge. Consequently, convergence is expected in facilitative areas of the law, whereas divergence due to different local preferences could be sustainable in interventionist areas of the law (areas of the law not subject to market pressure). This should be true so long as jurisdictions are unconstrained to adopt rules and have good information about the effects of alternative arrangements.

Divergences of legal systems are not necessarily a sign of inefficiency. There is no reason to think that there is only one single efficient rule for every legal problem. Yet, there are obstacles to convergence that result from local rent-seeking (essentially by the legal professions), legal culture and other forms of transaction costs.

In this context, harmonization that has often been justified on economic grounds (in the European Union, for example) has encountered a more hostile audience in legal economists. The clear preference for interjurisdictional competition and choice of law as a form to promote the emergence of efficient rules of law has found wide support in the economic literature. In fact, for example, hybrid legal systems are in a good position to benefit from the competition of different legal arrangements within a single jurisdiction.

c) Transplants

Legal transplants raise two significant economic questions. First, when will a given jurisdiction prefer to adopt a solution already available in a different jurisdiction rather than develop their own rule (incurring the possibility of "rediscovering the wheel")? The development of internal rules versus the adoption of transplants responds to a trade-off. Transplants provide benefits in terms of facilitating international interaction (economic or otherwise). They also generate internal costs in terms of legal consistency and local preferences. The existence of a strategic motivation that ignores externalities derived from the adoption of particular transplants might generate an inefficient level of transplant adoption.

The second question asks what legal systems or legal families are more prone to import or export successfully legal rules. It has been argued that the local conditions for transplanting and adopting a particular law are more important than the supply from a particular legal family. Predisposition and familiarity with the transplanted laws are more relevant than legal origin in assuring effective transplants.

d) Rule of law and development

Rule of law is expected to be associated with legal certainty, an independent judiciary and serious limitations to both private and state expropriation. A positive correlation is anticipated between a high adherence to rule of law, investment and measures of economic development. Generally, there is a strong relationship between rule of law and economic development. The reasons for such strong relationship, however, are debatable once one recognizes that the fastest growing economies today do not have an effective court system. The interaction between rule of law and economic development may be more complex than initially anticipated. To a large extent, the direction of causation is still unclear. The economic approach to rule of law and development has actually been criticized for not considering specific institutional and legal arrangements.

e) Public choice and lawmaking

Lawmaking varies across legal families. This raises an economic question: Is there a particular mix of statute law or codification with judge-made law that is more efficient? Depending on preferences, the role of precedent and idiosyncrasies of a particular legal system, different mixes of case law and statute law can be efficient.

Constitutional law and economics overlap significantly with public choice theory. The two fields share a focus on the role of rules in structuring and constraining decision making, shifting the debate from choice within rules to the choice of higher-order rules. Constitutions are generally viewed as devices for minimizing agency costs. By establishing structures that prevent capture by certain interest groups, constitutions can ensure superior governance. Another tradition emphasizes the role of constitutions in constraining intertemporal choice through some form of precommitment.

Public choice considerations look at the specific structure of lawmaking—codification versus judge-made law—in addition to customary law and international treaties. Scholars in public choice focus on the role of rules (which are rigid and specific), standards (which are less rigid, with a wider range of discretion, but are subject to exhaustive considerations) and principles (which are subject to general and nonexhaustive considerations), timing, private interests, capture and the political process.

Finally, the economic approach to conflicts of law does not see conflicts of law as a problem but rather as an opportunity to benefit from international jurisdictional and search for the appropriate legal rule across jurisdictions. The efficient solution to conflict of laws should internalize the externalities created by the interaction of individuals located in different jurisdictions. A strategy oriented to apply the legal rule of the jurisdiction where the harm has been produced is not always efficient since there might be important detrimental incentives.

f) Infrastructure of the legal system

Judges—Every legal system is based on an infrastructure of legal actors. As central actors in any legal system, judges are an understandable focus of economic analysis. One appropriate distinction is between "career" judiciaries, in which judges serve in a bureaucratic hierarchy for an entire career, and "recognition" judiciaries, in which judges are appointed to the bench relatively late in life. These systems can be distinguished as emphasizing different forms of monitoring agents: the career system emphasizes ex post controls on judicial decision making, while the recognition system involves ex ante screening of agents.

The incentives provided by different institutional audiences and the way different legal systems tackled them have been addressed from an economic perspective, particularly selection mechanisms. Such work has suggested a more nuanced approach than relying on the traditional common-law/civil-law distinction, examining micro-incentives, and distinguishing judiciaries even within the same legal tradition.

Lawyers—An economic perspective on the legal profession and the structure of law firms has looked at entry regulation, legal fees (the existence of contingent and conditional fees, in particular), organization of law firms, the regulation of publicity and information disclosure about legal services and rules of conduct.

Important differences in legal education and legal scholarship have been the object of economic analysis. Rather than relying exclusively on cultural preferences and path dependence, legal economists use a market approach and incentives to understand why legal education and the production of innovations in legal analysis have been persistently different across the world. A particular topic of interest is, for instance, the asymmetric influence of law and economics in legal thinking in different jurisdictions. Generally speaking, it is safe to say that law and economics has been more influential in North America than in other regions of the world, and this fact itself is an interesting question for analysis.

Prosecutors—There has been relatively less work on prosecutors by legal economists. In an under-resourced environment, one should expect that prosecutors will bring only the cases they are likely to win. A high conviction rate thus may provide insight into prosecutor incentives as well as judicial propensities. Risk aversion and career goals also vary across legal systems.

Chapter 4

THE LEGAL ORIGINS' THEORY[1]

Much literature suggests that the legal family that countries developed, imported or had involuntarily imposed on them had profound long-term effects on a range of economic outcomes. This approach is called "legal origins." This literature arose from the scholarly work of four economists known under the acronym LLSV—Rafael La Porta, Florencio López-de-Silanes, Andrei Shleifer and Robert Vishny.[2]

On a broader level, the legal origins' approach can be understood as being part of the more general quest by economists for institutional explanations for economic performance, particularly growth and development, following the seminar work by Douglas North (1990) and other economic historians.

The economic literature has proposed six factors to explain why a legal system could matter for economic growth: (1) the costs of identifying and applying efficient rules, (2) the system's ability to restrain rent-seeking in rule formulation and application, (3) the cost of adapting rules to changing circumstances, (4) the transaction costs to parties needing to learn the law, (5) the ease of contracting around rules and (6) the costs of transitions between systems. At the heart of the debate about the legal origins' theory is how these six factors relate in a meaningful way to legal families, though it remains largely undertheorized and generally, unanswered.

LLSV heavily relied on the categories devised by comparative law scholars to overcome the endogeneity problem that plagues most attempts to determine the causal relationship between law on the one hand and economic outcomes on the other. That is, in view of the statistical correlation (as shown by many studies) between "effective" legal institutions and economic development, one may be tempted to conclude that law causes economic development. However, the reverse is equally plausible, with effective legal institutions being a superior good whose desirability increases as countries become richer.

---

1 Extensive parts of this chapter follow from Garoupa and Pargendler (2014) and Garoupa and Ulen (2021). An excellent introduction to this literature can be found in Deakin and Pistor (2012).
2 A detailed summary is presented by La Porta et al. (2008).

In LLSV's econometric model, legal rules and institutions derived from certain legal families, which resulted from involuntary processes of conquest and colonization that took place in the distant past. Legal families could be deemed to be exogenous, which permitted the authors to conclude that legal institutions had a causal impact on economic outcomes, and not the other way around. Although the first studies in this literature used legal families as an instrumental variable in two-stage regressions, later studies abandoned that approach, as it became increasingly understood that legal families had a direct and independent effect on the variables of interest.

a) Efficiency of the common law hypothesis

In the mid- to late 1990s, LLSV studied financial development around the world and documented significant variance across legal protections offered to investors. According to LLSV, much of this variance could be traced to legal origins, with common-law countries providing more extensive investor protections than civil-law countries. Thus, it can be said that the legal origins' approach was initially a product of scholarship focused on financial economics. The legal origins' theory—that is, a complete explanation about the channels by which certain variance across relevant financial and economic variables is determined by legal families—would emerge somewhat later.

In searching for some theoretical background in law and economics for the initial insights of legal origins, some scholars have related the LLSV approach to two older discussions in the field, namely the so-called efficiency of the common law hypothesis and its cousin, "the inferiority of legislation in terms of economic efficiency." In the 1970s it was suggested that there is an implicit economic logic to the common law. What does that mean? The doctrines of the common law, as a whole, comprise consistent incentives that induce efficient behavior, not merely in market transactions, but in all social contexts. Because the original hypothesis lacked an explicit mechanism to explain the efficiency of the common law, a remarkable and extensive literature emerged in the late 1970s and 1980s seeking to provide that mechanism. With the legal origins' theory, the efficiency of the common law hypothesis regained attention, and new and important contributions were made in the 2000s.

Following Richard Posner's hypothesis (published in 1972), a long literature on the efficiency of the common law emerged; this literature is not comparative, strictly speaking, since it effectively looks only at judge-made law. Posner's original hypothesis does not entertain the proposition that a common-law system is more appropriate than a civil-law system in the evolution toward efficient rules.

This leap in reasoning requires two important steps. First, the argument must begin from the proposition that judge-made law is more efficient than statute law. Not all economists agree; for example, Gordon Tullock argued that capture by private interests and rent-seeking distorts the common-law, that is, the adversary system of dispute resolution and the judge-law process of rulemaking are mostly inefficient. A different system like that of the civil-law, based on statutes, is relatively less problematic because private capture and rent dissipation are less damaging within an inquisitorial dispute resolution mechanism and centralized rulemaking. Most economists disagree with Tullock.

Second, civil-law has been perceived as a legal system overwhelmingly statute dominated with no meaningful judge-made law. With these two additional steps, one can see the efficiency of the common law hypothesis as inspiring legal origins' theory. There is, of course, plenty of criticism to be made about the leap one just described, but it should not be ignored or underplayed.

b) Legal origins: LLSV

LLSV argued that legal origins explain a great deal of the variation in economic performance among countries. The general format of the legal origins' approach to their scholarship is easily summarized in two steps: first, show or explain the link between legal systems and certain laws or regulations; second, document that those specific laws or regulation are associated with variance in relevant outcomes across countries.

In their 2008 seminal review of the literature, the authors suggested three categories to understand their research. The first category of papers directly follows LLSV by examining some aspects of investor protection, corporate law or contract enforcement. The second category of papers looks at the link between legal origins and government regulation of economic activity and markets. The third category of papers debates the relationship between legal origins and features of legal institutions, such as the judiciary.

As scholars have emphasized, these broad categories of research have remained broadly consistent since the 2008 LLSV review. The main message today is still that common-law legal systems are statistically associated with more secure property rights, greater levels of judicial independence and superior financial development.

Many other scholars have published empirical studies in the last two decades inspired by the legal origins' theory but not directly related to the LLSV research agenda. These include the importance of legal origins to economic growth rates, successful legal transplants and economic development broadly understood. Others reviewed LLSV's scholarship by coming up with additional statistical results that challenge the common-law versus civil-law empirical relevance in certain contexts. For example, colonial history has emerged as an important challenge to legal origins. It has been said that that colonial history is a more relevant determinant of economic performance than is the legal origin.

Legal origins' theory has faced significant criticism from many economists in methodological grounds. For example, statistical analysis could be overstating the extent to which countries that share legal origins actually have similar substantive laws or legal institutions; it could be that the empirical results are determined by particular statistical coding rather than actual law. It is likely that the elected methodology is undermining other possible and more promising legal classifications—that is, different taxonomies that might be more successful in capturing legally relevant differences for purposes of understanding economic outcomes. Furthermore, it is not straightforward that old legal origins shape modern regulatory regimes; just consider that the common-law countries' economic success is too recent in time (after WWII), and certain areas of the law are shaped by new modern legal ideas.

More critical arguments against legal origins suggest that LLSV ignore systematic differences between countries that are likely to affect growth and that pre-date their legal origins, namely patterns of colonization and natural resources. It is also said that they fail to detect the mechanisms through which legal origins impact contemporary economic outcomes; they neglect significant legal developments, such as transplants, or understate other fundamental relevant determinants, such as culture.

c) Legal origins: Theory

The initial works by LLSV provided no clear theory. Later works by these and other authors have conceptualized two potential mechanisms to explain the empirical patterns observed by LLSV. The first one, the coined "adaptability channel," proposes that the common law is more effective in promoting financial markets (and possibly economic growth) because common-law judges have more power to adapt the law to economic needs. At the same time, civil-law judges are supposedly more constrained by codified principles. Comprehensive statutory codification undermines judicial ability to make law in new circumstances and where economic needs are pervasive. The "adaptability channel" evidently echoes the so-called efficiency of the common law hypothesis.

The second suggested mechanism is known as the "political channel." Here, the argument is that common-law emphasizes private property rights and contractual approaches while civil-law gives a greater play to social or collective rights and mandatory rules. Consequentially, common-law courts are more independent and more effective in restraining state expropriation, while civil-law courts are presumably weak in constraining executive power. In this reasoning, the efficiency of the common law-hypothesis is implicit; it only makes sense if courts are better than legislators at promoting law more conducive to economic growth.

As scholars have recognized, these two mechanisms are functionally the same. The "adaptability channel" only works if the "political channel" exists. Moreover, these two potential channels are introduced as exogenous mechanisms while, in fact, they are endogenous to the political process. In this light, these channels are themselves shaped by economic and social outcomes. If so, one might have an argument for reverse causality (inevitably undermining the alleged theoretical argument).

d) Legal origins: Critiques

The legal origins' theory has proven to be as controversial as it is influential. Despite its popularity, the criticisms both to its methodology and conclusions are numerous—in fact, too numerous to be addressed in full here. One will focus on only a few of the most conspicuous challenges to this line of inquiry. There is a growing literature, produced mostly by French legal scholars, that simply rejects efficiency as a relevant metric to compare different legal systems. Although specifically directed to the legal origins' theory, the criticism here is broader in nature; it applies to the entire field of law and economics and to any kind of economic-oriented argument. Researchers affiliated with this approach will invariably conclude that efficiency or other economic measures are inadequate in describing and evaluating legal regimes.

Other authors have attacked the legal origins' literature as a defective exercise in comparative law. Objections include the irrelevance or fluidity of legal family categories as well as the inherent difficulties in measuring legal institutions. Legal family categories were, without exception, designed by lawyers and for lawyers. The defining criteria of such classifications—such as the "sources of law"—are of interest to legal scholars and lawyers, but hardly relevant for most questions that are the object of social science research. In fact, these categorizations had didactic purposes and did not seek to accurately describe the laws of affiliate legal systems. Konrad Zweigert and Hein Kötz in 1987, go so far as to urge comparative law scholars to focus on the larger legal family. Relatedly, comparative law scholars have always regarded the defining criteria for legal family categories, as well as the classification of individual countries under one group or another, as highly problematic.

Arguably, these legal families are unbefitting variables, for example, statistical regressions or social science explanations more broadly.

Nevertheless, the use of legal families by economists relies on the assumption that such groupings have deep historical (and exogenous) roots. It is revealing that what comparative lawyers call "legal families" economists have come to term "legal origins," an expression that highlights the purported historicity of these categories that is key to their proponents' purposes. Not only did the relevant classifications undergo significant change over time, but also the comparativists who designed them explicitly recognized that their taxonomies were temporally grounded.

Moreover, the view of law as a "politically neutral endowment" reflected in the legal origins' literature has also come under attack. For example, some of the most significant differences in corporate governance and capital market development across jurisdictions are arguably due to context-specific political developments in the twentieth century. There is also evidence that at least some countries voluntarily picked and chose their rules of commercial law ever since the nineteenth century, thereby challenging the view that legal origins are necessarily exogenous.

Studies on the relationship between law and development carry an implicit assumption: law and legal institutions matter a great deal for economic outcomes. Inevitably this is an empirical question. Not surprisingly, many authors have focused on the particular econometrics to criticize the legal origins' literature. A number of studies have provided countervailing empirical evidence to challenge the claim that common-law is superior to civil-law from an economic standpoint. These works identify the advantages of civil-law over common-law institutions, show reversals in the patterns of financial development across legal traditions over time and find that other variables are superior to legal origins in predicting economic outcomes.

Last, but not least, even if one were to accept the conclusions of econometric studies showing the purported advantages of common-law institutions, the inquiry would remain incomplete without identifying the mechanisms and channels that account for the superiority of the common-law system.

e) Legal origins: Importance in law and economics

LLSV's research had a significant and enduring impact in economics broadly defined. Applications range from growth in GDP per capita, use of military conscription, climate change policies, criminal incarceration to judicial decisions in Europe.

Before the influential LLSV scholarship, there was a small literature intersecting the common-law/civil-law distinction with specific law and economics applications in a few areas of the law.[3] The development and growing popularity of the legal origins in the early 2000s had a significant impact on law and economics as a field. First, as mentioned earlier, it reopened the interest in the "efficiency of the common law" hypothesis with a new wave of formal models and empirical studies. It also advanced the literature by showing that the efficiency of the common law requires a complex set of assumptions that are debatable, either because they are unrealistic or because they are unlikely to be satisfied most of the time.

Second, the cold reception that legal origins received from comparatists and their critical response to its significance generated a debate in law and economics about the relevance of the common-law/civil-law distinction for explaining differences in economic growth and financial markets. In particular, legal economists have focused on the macrostructure of legal institutions (e.g., the judiciary and courts) and constitutional issues.

Finally, applications and additional empirical legal studies have inevitably emerged to fill the gap between legal origins, quantitative comparative law and more micro-based traditional law and economics.

Consider a recent example—transmission rates of HIV in Africa (Anderson 2018). The general idea of Anderson's paper is that African countries' legal origins are correlated with aspects of their legal systems like property rights, and that those differences are in turn correlated with HIV incidence. The author argues that, under common-law marital property law, women have less bargaining power in the family and are in a weaker position to secure safe sex; thus, they are more vulnerable. In contrast, under civil-law marital property law, women are in a stronger position in the household and can impose safe sex, thus reducing the incidence of HIV.

Here is a second example—organ donation laws (Riambau et al. 2020), and presumed consent (an opt-out system) versus explicit consent (an opt-in system). Civil-law seems to predict presumed consent regimes, controlling for other variables. The authors argue that legal origins, while pre-dating transplantation medicine by two centuries, seem influential nowadays (even after controlling for religion). Their reasoning is that civil-law reveals a preference for state allocation policies whereas common-law reflects a preference for private allocation mechanisms.

Although the legal origins' literature has also been the subject of a highly contested academic debate, the common-law/civil-law dichotomy is now regularly used as a control variable in any empirical study about growth or development, or cross-country empirical work more generally. In fact, it

---

3 See the examples discussed by Mattei (1998).

is inconceivable now that any serious cross-country empirical work related to economic performance will forget to consider the common-law/civil-law dummy variable. Economists are definitely divided about how far legal origins reflect current institutions or shape recent economic outcomes, but the importance of LLSV's insights is widely recognized.

Chapter 5

COMPARATIVE PRIVATE
LAW AND ECONOMICS[1]

The starting point of a microeconomic analysis of comparative law must be the Coase Theorem, introduced by Ronald Coase (1960). Before his article, economists largely argued that externalities (external effects to market transactions), such as pollution, should be addressed by appropriate taxation (requiring government intervention). Coase refocused the analysis by emphasizing the role of bargaining and transaction costs in determining efficiency within a certain entitlement imposed by law. In a world of zero transaction costs and well-defined legal rules (plus a few other less important technical assumptions), a Coasian bargaining guarantees efficiency. In such a world, law is about specifying initial entitlements, guaranteeing costless enforcement and achieving redistribution (since initial entitlements do not affect efficient outcomes but do shape redistribution). However, in a world with transaction costs, different legal regimes may have varying consequences on the efficiency of outcomes. Transaction costs are the costs of making and enforcing the transaction of initial entitlements. Examples include negotiation costs and agency costs (monitoring, enforcement and avoidance).

Consider Kaldor–Hicks efficiency. In a very general way, this principle suggests that changes in legal policy are efficient if gains exceed or potentially compensate losses. Thus, after exhausting all possible modifications that satisfy the Kaldor–Hicks principle, the emerging law should maximize social welfare (i.e., aggregate wealth). However, unlike the Pareto principle, the Kaldor–Hicks approach does not claim consensual exchanges. The Pareto principle demands that no one can be made better off without making someone else worse off. Therefore, if there are Pareto improvements (making someone better without making someone else worse), social welfare has not been optimized. However, Kaldor–Hicks efficiency guarantees that social

---

1 Extensive parts of this chapter follow from Garoupa (2018), Acciarri and Garoupa (2013), Garoupa et al. (2017) and Garoupa and Ginsburg (2012).

welfare is maximized, but not that everyone is in a better-off world. It shows that, under the most efficient law, the winners could potentially compensate the losers. It has been said that the Kaldor–Hicks principle is about implied consent, thus replacing actual consent under Pareto efficiency.

a) Property law and economics: Brief overview

From the viewpoint of law and economics, property law should be designed to ensure maximization of property value, both in terms of transactions and use as collateral for capital market development. Moreover, following the basic insight of Coase (1960), the establishment of adequate entitlements and the adoption of legal rules that reduce transaction costs will help in the necessary bargaining to internalize externalities.

Under consensual transfer of property, in a world of costless information, rules should favor the original owner. Therefore, a property rule prevails—all transfers are voluntary and require some form of consent. However, since information is costly, legal protection of original ownership should be incomplete. If so, a liability rule could be efficient—involuntary transfer is allowed occasionally, but the original owner should be compensated. Therefore, when facing competing claims by the current possessor and a claimant (presumably the original owner), protection of property titling must balance incentives (possible moral hazard concerns) and risk sharing. The result may require a combination of rules (e.g., a pliability rule—an entitlement protected by a property rule if some conditions apply turns into a liability rule when such conditions disappear). For example, the treatment of a bona fide purchase must consider the costs of prevention (by the original owner) against the costs of titling search (by the new buyer), thus resulting in complex arrangements.

The law and economics of property emphasizes consensual exchange as the primary mechanism in achieving allocative efficiency. Nonconsensual transfers attract attention when there are high transaction costs or significant externalities. Adverse possession, for example, should be understood in this context. It is a form of coercive transfer of property between private individuals. However, it does provide for important incentives—it deters the owner from neglecting the property and it reduces uncertainty over time (by arranging for statutory limitations).

Government takings are also an interesting example. Law and economics introduces an economic meaning to "just compensation." The compensation cannot be too low, because it would foster too many takings (since the government would not bear the actual cost of a taking) and underinvestment in development by current landowners. The compensation cannot be too high (full compensation) because there would be overinvestment in development (moral hazard). A possible effective rule would be no compensation is paid if the taking is efficient and full compensation should be paid if the taking is inefficient.

The fact that property law varies across jurisdictions has naturally attracted the attention of legal economists to assess the extent to which certain aspects of property law are more or less efficient. A fundamental issue is of course titling of property around the world—namely, recording versus registration. One other significant topic is the rise of anticommons (i.e., a single resource with numerous rights holders who can prevent others from using it by opposition to commons, a single resource with too many users) and its consequences for property market and investment.

b) Property law and economics: Bona fide purchase

Consider the following situation: a farmer buys cattle from a person who does not have a good title. The true owner wants the cattle back after this transaction has taken place. At this point, both the farmer, who has paid for the cattle in good faith, and the true owner seem to have strong claims of ownership.

In French law, like most civil law systems, good faith possession of movables produces a good title, even in situations where the bona fide purchaser acquires his right from someone without any right (in cases of *adquisitio a non domino*). The traditional common law rule has been that no one can have a better title than the title one rightfully owns (*nemo plus iura in alium transferre potest quam ipse habet* or *nemo dat quod non habet*). Therefore, mere current possession of property is not conclusive of title under English law, although it could be under French law and other civil law systems. The English law approach protects the interests of the current rightful owner against the fraud committed by third parties who sell a good that is lacking rightful authorization. The rule entitles the owner to recover the property from an innocent purchaser. Consequently, the innocent purchaser cannot rely on the fact of having acquired the good from a seller under good faith.

Under English law, the original owner seems to be in a better position to claim ownership than the farmer; under French law, by contrast, the farmer could have an advantage. These two rules generate a very different ex ante allocation of property rights and incentives. The *nemo dat* rule, followed by traditional English law, avoids theft, since the person who acquires from the thief has no possible action against the true owner's claim. The French rule, which protects the bona fide purchaser independently of the origin of the movable, reduces the investigation costs the potential purchaser must carry out. Under French law, the original owner must bear higher prevention costs to avoid the cattle being taken; otherwise, the likelihood of recovery is low.

Under English law, the farmer must spend more resources in investigating the quality of the ownership status of the seller. When the costs of prevention of theft are high, the English rule (*nemo dat*) is more efficient. By the same token, if the information costs concerning the right of the conveyor are significant, the French solution is more desirable.

In general, one expects prevention costs to be lower than title quality investigation costs. Thus, one could argue that the French rule promotes market exchange, whereas the English rule delays or deters that exchange. This is a good micro illustration where the French rule is presumably more efficient (or at least more market friendly) than traditional common law.

The effect of such a rule seems clear. Under the traditional common-law rule, owners can be confident in their ability to recover property that has been conveyed without their allowance. At the same time, potential purchasers of goods must always be aware of the identity of the seller and the validity of her right to sell. Obviously, the problem is more acute with movable property.

The weaker the protection that the bona fide purchaser has, the more important the proof and quality of title is to the purchaser. This increases the cost of each purchase in the economy, potentially hurting trade. Such effect has forced many common law jurisdictions to restrict the extent to which current owners are protected. The nature of the market and the necessity of conducting quick and secure deals have introduced corrections to the protection of owners and have effectively brought the common-law rule closer to the French solution.

One now adds the observation of the legal origins' literature to this analysis: the French rule is enforced less effectively than the traditional English rule. The true original owner is the individual who needs an enforceable rule since the buyer has the possession of the good. Therefore, less effective enforcement of the French rule does not generate a major loss of efficiency, whereas more effective enforcement of the English rule increases the costs of investigation for the buyer. In fact, weaker enforcement is not a good method for ranking the efficiency of property law across legal families because it implicitly assumes that the substantive rules are equivalent, and only the degree to which they are enforced makes a difference. As one has seen with the example of bona fide purchasing, that is a misguided assumption.

c) **Property law and economics: Titling**

Property rights are conveyed because of an exchange among people. Consequently, it is crucial to determine who owns the right to control a certain resource or a specific good. At the same time, it is important to discover the ability of the owner to transmit or limit the use of the resource. This problem is common to movable property as well as real estate property. In the case of real estate property, given its costs and use as collateral in modern economics, it is more relevant to identify the owner and to know the legal status of the property in order to protect purchasers. It is easy to understand that, in every legal system, a great part of the rules governing real estate property are intended to promote a reliable way to convey and exchange property. The main goal involves the protection of potential purchasers and their ability to get loans. As it is well known, real estate security and stability play a role of the utmost importance in economic growth.

In this context, another good example in property law of the critical difference between common-law and civil-law systems is the titling system of land, namely recording versus registration. In very broad terms, France uses a recording system, whereas registration prevails in England. The main difference between the two is that recording does not generate a provisional priority for claims, whereas registration does. Consequently, in the case of a valid claim by a third party, the current owner keeps the land under registration (the rightful claimant gets compensated by the public system of registration), whereas under recording, the current owner loses the land (but usually receives compensation if an insurance mechanism is in place).

In this context, the American case does not provide a good benchmark. Both systems coexist in the United States (e.g., Cook County in the state of Illinois). Each state has adopted a register of deeds that aims to give potential purchasers and lenders constructive notice about the legal status of the property. More generally, the American legal system, based on the general principle of the relativity of titles, does not provide any kind of previous control or examination of the registered deeds. Under the traditional rule of the common law, however, the superiority of one claim to another should be determined by temporal ordering. The situation is quite different in many civil-law systems, such as Germany or Spain, where land registries and ex ante controls over the legality and validity of deeds promote a safer system to convey real estate property.

The alleged superiority of the registration system is not immune to criticism. Registration helps property transactions, as well as the use of property as collateral, by reducing uncertainty. However, it is a more expensive and demanding system because the cost of purging titles is not negligible. Consequently, it could be that a more expensive system, such as registration, expels an important fraction of property from the public system. On the other hand, recording is a cheaper titling system, and therefore the fraction of property expelled from the public system is presumably lower. Clearly, there is a trade-off between the assurance of quality of titling in land and the expulsion of property from the public system. From a theoretical perspective, it is not clear which titling system is better for the enforcement of property rights. Given the economic importance of titling systems for property and credit markets, there are good reasons to be cautious about endorsing the view that French law is inadequate. In this context, the pure common-law/civil-law distinction does not seem to be a relevant dimension for assessing the quality of titling of property.

d) Contract law and economics: Brief overview

Law and economics develops the perspective that contractual parties engage in mutually beneficial exchanges that are efficient in nature. Contracts are stipulated to enhance the occurrence of such transfers. However, since they take place in a context of imperfect or asymmetric information, it is possible that at some point the social benefits do not justify the social costs of performance, raising the possibility of optimal breach. Law and economics explores the extent to which remedies for nonperformance induce optimal breach, in particular specific performance and damages.

Courts should adopt contractual remedies that promote breach only when it is efficient to do so. Unlimited expectation damages are usually inefficient because they generate incentives for appropriate reliance but also inappropriate risk sharing. Therefore, limited expectation damages are usually better. By the same reasoning, mere reliance damages are generally insufficient. Specific performance emerges as an efficient remedy for specific assets (i.e., unique goods and services) because it tends to lower transaction costs and protect subjective value. Liquidated damages are an example of a remedy negotiated by the parties. Since court-designed remedies are costly to enforce and require information (i.e., courts make mistakes), law and economics suggests that liquidated damages should be enforced, since they support credible commitment by the parties and reflect an effort to maximize the value of the contract.

Disclosure rules are one important aspect of contractual law and thus deserve attention by legal economists. Since asymmetric information might undermine efficient transactions or promote inefficient exchanges, disclosure of information is relevant. However, the nature of the information matters for assessing rules. For example, casually acquired information makes the disclosure rule irrelevant for efficiency. The opposite example is deliberately acquired information (which presupposes some cost). Purely distributive information should require disclosure (at the penalty of rescinding), while socially valuable information should not require disclosure (contract should be enforced). These rules enhance the production of socially useful information while discouraging a costly search for purely distributive information.

In particular, mandatory rules of disclosure make information a public good, hence generating suboptimal contracts.

The question of monetary damages versus specific performance has deserved attention from a comparative perspective. Traditionally, Anglo-American legal systems tended to prefer monetary damages, whereas civil-law jurisdictions seemed to favor specific performance, even under conditions that make it unlikely to be efficient. Other important issues in comparative contract law that have deserved attention from legal economists include pre-contractual liability in the context of the efficient breach theory, disclosure of information prior to contract formation and regulation of cooling-off periods.

e) Tort law and economics: Brief overview

The economic perspective on torts looks at the most efficient way of deterring accidents or wrongdoings. Remedies and liability rules are assessed from the perspective of the benefit in avoiding accidents or tort wrongdoings (hence, deterring their occurrence) and the cost of prevention. Compensation of victims is discussed from the perspective of internalizing accident costs and providing the adequate ex ante incentives to potential tortfeasors.

The economic literature uses the unilateral care model for pedagogical reasons. Suppose an injurer spends a dollar in precaution. The probability of an accident varies with precaution while the victim suffers damage. The social optimum would be a level of precaution that minimizes its cost plus the expected damage for the victim. Under a no-liability rule, the injurer would spend zero dollars, which is clearly inefficient. Therefore, strict liability emerges as an efficient solution since it forces the injurer to internalize the costs of wrongdoing. What about negligence rules? They are trivially optimal in the unilateral care model because there is only one source of causation—the injurer's behavior. These results can be framed under the Hand Rule formulated by Judge Learned Hand in 1947. He argued that if the burden (of avoiding a wrongdoing) is less than the expected damage imposed on the victim, then the injurer should be liable.

Different negligence rules can be assessed in the bilateral care model. Strict liability is no longer efficient since it creates a moral hazard problem (victim free rides on the injurer's compensation). Contributory negligence is now economically more sensible since it balances the injurer's costs of precaution against the victim's cost of avoiding an accident. It turns out that the final result depends on the due care standard (i.e., the switch point between liability and no liability for the injurer). If correctly specified, it can be proved that a contributory negligence rule is efficient.

Extensions of the basic accident model (activity levels, participation costs, learning, different forms of causation, scope of liability and judgment-proof issues) complicate the analysis and highlight that both strict liability and different negligence rules (contributory negligence, strict liability with contributory negligence, comparative negligence, sharing negligence and other variations) have efficiency shortcomings. For example, while strict liability does not require any particular knowledge about the appropriate due care standard, a negligence rule requires a court that is not prone to error. Without estimation of the injurer's actual precaution and due care standard being both accurate, a negligence rule inevitably introduces legal error—false positives (wrong convictions) and false negatives (wrong acquittals). These additional costs of legal error must be added to the costs of prevention.

Punitive damages have attracted attention by legal economists. As opposed to compensatory damages, punitive damages exceed the harm suffered by the victim. The economic rationale is that compensation to the victim is not certain. Therefore, to impose the correct cost–benefit analysis to the injurer, expected damages might have to equal the harm. Under such condition, actual damages should equal the harm divided by the probability of paying damages (the well-known "multiplier principle"). Punitive damages, in this analysis, play the adequate role of capturing the less-than-one probability of paying damages faced by the injurer.

A related issue is the decoupling between damages paid by the injurer and award received by the victim. The economic reasoning is clear—there are two goals (setting the levels of precaution for both injurer and victim) and one instrument (level of compensation). Therefore, the possibility of separating damages and awards emerges as a viable solution. The more controversial discussion is about the institutional setup to address the difference between what the injurer pays and what the victim receives, when positive (damages are taxed and split between victim and government) or negative (requires a subsidy by the government to the victim).

In a more comparative law analysis, Anglo-American tort doctrines have been compared to the civil law of obligations, and the way incentives are shaped in that context has been debated. Among the relevant topics addressed in the economic literature are tort law, product liability, the different approaches to strict liability and negligence rules across jurisdictions (e.g., the Good Samaritan rule, mitigation of damages, and last clear chance), quasi-contracts, *gestion d'affaires* (a particular form of quasi-contract under French law by which the actions of one individual benefit another individual), the principle of *non-cumul* in contractual and tort liability (under French law, contractual and tort liability cannot be challenged at the same time) and pure economic losses (with traditional limited recovery).

Torts are negative externalities; hence, the focus of an economic analysis is on liability rules that force injurers and victims to act efficiently. There are positive externalities, though negative liability rarely exists (for instance, as regulated by the law of restitution). The explanation is mainly administrative costs. Transaction costs and potential coordination issues may justify why restitution is limited.

f) Contract and tort law and economics: The principle of non-cumul

Suppose a certain breach of contract creates a potentially tortious wrongdoing. A relevant legal question is the extent to which this breach of contract can be a cause of action concurrently in torts and contracts. For example, consider situations where breach of contract causes physical or emotional harm to the injured party. Historically, product liability claims have generated the need for such a legal solution. Such situations posed the problem that the existence of a contract might ban the application of tort remedies. Tort remedies were designed for the absence of a previous relation among the tortfeasor and the injured party. At the same time, legal remedies for breach of contract might be insufficient because the physical and emotional harm suffered by the victim is not one of the foreseeable outcomes in the context of a typical contractual relation.

There are a few cases where the injured party is forced to strategically choose to pursue breach of contract under contractual liability or other liability, for example, in restitution. However, in most cases, when the same harm or impairment can be regarded as either contract or tort, there are no general legal provisions. Nevertheless, a contract cannot always generate a tort claim. For purposes of the present discussion, one assumes that there are particular situations when an injured party could strategically choose between pursuing compensation by contractual liability or by tort liability: a "picking the theory" choice.

Such situations raise two different, though related, questions. First, does the victim have two different claims against the same agent, one based on contractual remedies for breach of contract, and another based on tort liability rules? Second, and if so, then can the victim claim both in the same cause of action? It is universally accepted that, in any case, the victim cannot recover twice for the same harm or detriment.

Traditional civil-law codes have disregarded these complex questions. Therefore, they have been addressed by case law. In that respect, the problems related to the coexistence of tort and contract claims are a good field to compare the approaches by civil and common-law. In both cases, the rules have their origin in judge-made law; hence, there are no structural differences in the process used to reach the legal solution—common-law courts, as well as civil-law judges, have selected the best solution in their own understanding. The latter, like the former, have done so without a general and preceding statutory rule.

Apparently the American and English regimes are more flexible in that respect. The traditional English rule, which holds that contractual and tort claims should not be filed in the same cause of action, was overruled in 1995. Before this decision, concurrent liability in both contract and tort had been accepted in claims for physical injury only. The 1995 ruling opened the possibility for financial losses to the plaintiff. This ruling allowed one party to the contract to sue the other party for negligence in performing the contract, in addition to contractual remedies for breach of contract.

In the same way, German and Italian solutions tend to consider tort and contract rules on damages as mutually complementary. The case is clearer in Germany, where the doctrine and case law have defined the situation as an *Anspruchkonkurrenz*—that is to say, the coexistence of different rules aiming at a similar goal (although not identical since the same type of damage cannot be recovered twice).

The problem is not only a formal one regarding how to sum up a specific claim. The question relates to the boundaries of the right of the victim (either of harm or of breach of contract) to recover damages, due to the different ways to consider contractual and tort damages in most of the legal systems. It is clear that the wider the definition of tort is, the more important it is to limit it in order to avoid its accumulation with other claims, significantly those related with a contract. From this point of view, it seems obvious that the French system has developed the opposite solution. Different from the aforementioned rules, under the French principle of non-cumul, a victim of breach of contract cannot pursue a tort claim concurrently; when an obligation exists by virtue of a contract, it cannot also exist in tort.

As stated, the doctrine of non-cumul is a natural consequence of the definition of a tort under article 1382 of the French Civil Code: "Any act whatever of man, which causes damage to another, obliges the one by whose fault it occurred, to compensate it." Independent of doctrinal and historical explanations, it is disputable that the common-law rule of accumulation of contractual and noncontractual claims (also followed by some civil-law jurisdictions) promotes more efficient results than the French doctrine of non-cumul.

An efficiency approach should consider obligations contracted by mutual consent over other obligations. This principle underlies both the efficient formation and efficient breach of contracts. As a general principle, the use of tort law concurrently with contract law should be limited to specific situations where, for different reasons, one suspects contractual damages are unable to achieve the correct outcome. In other words, the efficient solution should look like a general principle of noncumulative contractual and tort obligations with some particular derogation. Those familiar with contract law around the world will immediately recognize that this general rule looks more similar to French law than to English, American or German laws.

The option for a principle of non-cumul seems wise from an economic point of view. First, obligations freely negotiated should supersede potential tortious wrongdoings. Second, the possibility that breach of contract could generate a tort claim undermines efficient breach. Third, *ex ante facto*, a potential tort claim could deter formation of contracts or increase negotiation costs to overcome potential future tort claims. Consequently, allowing tort claims concurrent with breach of contract claims can only be efficient in very exceptional conditions. One example is when contractual damages are unable to internalize the losses of nonperformance due to externalities or the existence of serious asymmetries of information that undermine the optimality of contractual rules.

One must also consider the long-term effects of the different rules. Suppose there is an important type of breach of contract that generates significant losses of a tortious nature. If the claims can never be the subject of action concurrently in torts and in contracts, one expects the evolution of the law to include this class in a broader scope of contract law. Even if they are tortious in nature, the fact that they are a byproduct of a contract and should only be cause of action in contract law is likely to be appropriate, because they are now subject to the mutual consent test. If they can be causes of action concurrently in torts and in contracts, there would be no evolutionary pressure to subject them to a mutual consent test.

In French law, where non-cumul is the rule, a large body of law has evolved under contract law over the years to extend *responsabilité contractuelle* to include actions that are substantively like tort law. Due to the non-cumul, such rules are housed within contract law. In other words, it seems that either the legal system sticks to the non-cumul under French law and accepts the growth of responsabilité contractuelle or the system decides that these cases must be dealt with as tort law cases despite the presence of a contractual relationship.

The expansion of responsabilité contractuelle because of the non-cumul is not without costs. The potential inclusion of actions of a tortious nature in responsabilité contractuelle creates a difficult balance for civil courts. Courts must assure that responsabilité contractuelle is, by and large, moving along the same lines as *responsabilité délictuelle* to deal effectively with cases that look more like torts than anything else (e.g., an injury to a contracting party while executing a contract). Developing and administering that body of law has a significant cost. Obviously, that cost can be minimized by keeping the two liability regimes close to one another; however, by then, the basic rule of non-cumul is consequently unnecessary.

Recognizing that the inclusion of actions of a tortious nature is likely to raise important questions in contract law, one is inclined to argue that the route taken by French law seems better, even from a dynamic perspective. The view is based on the nature of explicit mutual consent in contracts. The only exceptions should be damage situations that require high transaction costs to achieve mutual consent ex ante. Inserting these cases into a broader contractual responsibility would raise the problems of quasi-contracts, either by diluting the definition of mutual consent or by increasing the costs of contractual formation since those transaction costs become part of the costs of contract formation.

From an economic perspective, the conclusion is that the French model of a general principle of non-cumul, subject to particular derogations in order to address significant externalities, is more appropriate from both a static and dynamic perspective when compared to the solutions developed in the common-law and civil-law jurisdictions.

g) Tort law and economics: The Good Samaritan principle

The Good Samaritan principle or rule provides another example of how the common-law and civil-law differ in their approaches and impacts on efficiency. The relevance of this example is likely marginal since it does not have immediate economic effects. However, it provides a good exercise in the context of our discussion. The approach toward a duty to rescue varies under the common and civil-law; while civil-law systems tend to impose a duty to rescue to everyone, the traditional common-law solution foresees a no-duty-to-rescue rule.

Under the realm of traditional common-law rules, there is no affirmative duty to rescue another person from a situation of danger; Anglo-American courts do not impose a duty to rescue on bystanders. The rule has few exceptions and is almost universally accepted—exceptions are roughly related to situations of risk negligently created by the potential rescuer or with the existence of a special relationship between the potential rescuer and the rescuee. In most cases, no person has an obligation to save another, even when the probability of salvation is high, and its costs are small. Therefore, the lack of a duty to rescue creates an immediate disincentive to rescue: those who might want to rescue somebody in a risky situation may not carry out those dangerous activities after all. Those risky activities, however, can be socially beneficial.

The traditional civil-law approach differs from the traditional common-law rule. Under the civil-law, there is a general duty to rescue persons in danger, but the rescuee has to pay the rescuer for the expenses of the salvation. The duty to rescue, the Good Samaritan rule, is even enforced in the context of criminal law. This general rule has few exceptions, and all of them relate to situations where it is more than foreseeable that the rescue will be unsuccessful. The duty is not imposed where the cost of the rescue is excessive, although this exception is seldom used when the danger involves a natural person. In doing so, civil-law systems impose a liability rule on the potential rescuer, who will be liable if the rescue is not performed. It also imposes another liability rule to the rescuee, who must reward or reimburse the rescuer with the expenses of the rescue.

Clearly, the civil-law solution is superior and provides a more efficient framework to secure an implicit negotiation with high transaction costs. The two-sided liability rule promotes rescues that can be performed at a low cost, but at the same time generates incentives for taking precautionary action, since the person in peril knows that she must pay for the costs of her own rescue. Both actors are fully incentivized to perform adequately, from both individual and social perspectives.

Notice, however, that these rules tend to be irrelevant if individuals are altruist in their nature. If rescuers decide on the notion that there are moral or human obligations to rescue, the duty to rescue does not produce relevant consequences.

h) Economics of civil procedure: Brief overview

There is a serious divergence between the private and the social motivation to litigate. Each party cares about the estimated benefit from litigation and the respective private costs. Society cares about the extent to which litigation incentivizes compliance with the law and helps the development of the legal system through articulating efficient rules. From this perspective, the rules of civil procedure and the institutional framework where litigation takes place should reduce transaction costs (thus favoring cheaper out-of-court settlements) and align the private interests of the litigants with the social welfare-maximizing goals.

Litigation itself generates transaction costs. From an economic viewpoint, the puzzling question is why trials occur. Plaintiff and defendant save on trial costs if they reach a settlement out of court, but settlements do not always occur. There are two explanations for why few cases end up in trial. Litigants may have different opinions about the outcome of trial (e.g., optimism bias) or they may have private information about the case (a standard case of asymmetric information). Both models point to the same reasoning—a disagreement between plaintiff and defendant that undermines the possibility of a settlement.

Procedural rules, such as pretrial discovery or standard of proof, can be assessed within the two models of litigation. In the context of differing perceptions, procedural rules should be used to promote convergence of beliefs and facilitate settlement. In the context of asymmetric information, procedural rules should be evaluated in the extent to which they approximate information sets. For example, disclosure of evidence promotes convergence of beliefs and reduces asymmetry of information. However, it could also dissuade production of evidence by plaintiff or defendant.

One should point out that settlements have intrinsic costs that should not be ignored in a more comprehensive analysis. Disputes in trial are important for the development of common law, for example. They may also be relevant for a general perception of the law and codes of social conduct. Therefore, the elimination of trials is not an optimal policy. A similar reasoning applies to alternative dispute resolution mechanisms. They may save costs and enhance the quality of adjudication. However, they may have a negative impact on legal development (a problem enhanced if outcomes are subject to confidentiality).

The regulation of class actions is also relevant. In many situations, the individual expected benefit from filing a lawsuit is too low, which could be a concern (because it fails to discipline potential defendants). The possibility of class actions internalizes this collective action problem by lowering participation costs and reallocating authority to one individual (the lawyer forming the class). The disadvantages of class actions include the potential misalignment between plaintiffs and lawyer, the asymmetric information within the litigant group, and the possibility of frivolous lawsuits.

Appeals are justified from an economic perspective as a means of error correction as well as a mechanism for improving lawmaking. When appeals are not allowed, possible trial errors go uncorrected. However, if appeals are allowed with no restriction, litigants might use them as part of a strategy to postpone legal obligations. Therefore, an appeal system should be understood as a separating device. Litigation costs, procedure and rules of evidence need to be adjusted to address correction of errors in a cost-effective way.

i) Economics of civil procedure: Cost-shifting rules

The allocation of costs is critically important for civil litigation to explain the decision to file lawsuits and settlements rates. In the UK, the English rule largely prevails. The general rule is that the unsuccessful party will be ordered to pay the costs of the successful party. However, the award of costs at the conclusion of a case is at the discretion of the court. The discretion extends to whether the costs are payable by one party to another, the amount of those costs, and when they are to be paid. In deciding what order to make about costs, the court must give regard to all the circumstances, including the conduct of the parties.

In Canada, a rule of cost shifting in litigation by which the loser in a civil lawsuit must compensate the winner for a portion of the latter's legal costs is also applied. Generally speaking, costs do not amount to full compensation, and the proportion of the winner's legal bill covered by an award of costs typically decreases over time as legal fees continue to rise. Yet, since the nature of the rule remains informal and discretionary, litigants cannot fully rely upon its application when deciding whether to litigate. The decision to award costs is made at the conclusion of the action, which means a plaintiff still risks a substantial loss if the claim is ultimately unsuccessful.

In contrast, in the United States, each side generally bears its own costs, the so-called American rule. Notice that the English rule prevailed in the United States until the nineteenth century. The American rule was developed as lawyers gained the power to negotiate their contracts in a fairly unregulated framework. It became dominant by the 1850s. However, variants of a loser-pays-all rule still exist in federal civil procedure, namely Rule 68 of Federal Rules of Civil Procedure. Under this rule, a party might have to reimburse the costs of the other party if the award is less than a rejected offer of settlement (a similar rule has been adopted in England and Wales after the Woolf reforms to civil procedure in 1998). In many cases, the court is allowed to order the losing side to pay the legal costs of the winner; however, this is often subject to the discretion of the judge.

The English rule tends to prevail in common-law jurisdictions. The United States deviated from the general trend in the nineteenth century. The evolution of the rules concerning cost allocation could be a good example of multiple equilibria where the final outcome is determined by local determinants. The different structure of the legal markets, the practice of contingency fees (largely confined to the United States until recently), and the needs posed by different rates of growing civil litigation could easily determine the appropriate use of different rules.

There is extensive economic literature on the American versus English rule in civil litigation. As one has seen, under the American rule, each side pays their own legal costs. Under the English rule, the loser pays all. Under Rule 68 of the Federal Rules of Civil Procedure, a plaintiff who rejects a formal settlement offer by the defendant and later obtains a less favorable judgment pays the defendant's legal costs (post offer). Which of these rules promotes settlements? Rule 68 is clearly designed to favor settlements by making trial more costly to the plaintiff. Still, it also shifts the settlement amount in favor of defendants. The English versus American rule depends on the specifics of the analysis. If plaintiff and defendant are extremely optimistic, one should expect more trials under the English rule (because both sides think the legal costs will be borne by the other side). However, if both plaintiff and defendant exhibit significant aversion to risk, the American rule might induce more trials (since both sides are exposed to less risk). However, once legal costs are endogenous to the rules for allocating legal expenses, the analytics are complex and are driven by varying parameters.

Theoretical literature gives no consensus concerning the overall effect of shifting litigation costs. The controversial topics include the extent to which shifting costs promote settlement, enhance civil litigation, favor more meritorious claims or decrease the number of nuisance lawsuits. The results depend on asymmetric information, risk aversion, strategic positions and other procedural rules. The empirical and experimental literature is not conclusive.

Another important topic in this context is the use of contingent fees for paying lawyers. More generally, the rules for allocating costs between the plaintiff and the plaintiff's lawyers also affect the outcome of litigation. When a fixed fee regulates the relationship between plaintiff and lawyer, the lawyer is paid regardless of the outcome. Under a contingent fee, a percentage (usually one-third) of the award goes to the lawyer. The lawyer gets zero if the plaintiff loses (no win, no fee). A conditional fee usually involves a flat payment plus a percentage of the recovery. Economists like contingent fee arrangements because of incentives to work (avoid shirking), risk sharing, and access to justice (they allow poor plaintiffs to pursue lawsuits by using the value of the potential award as a collateral). However, there are concerns— issues with settlement, since both sides share risk (mainly, allocation of settlement authority), possibility of frivolous suits (because plaintiffs ignore the full cost of trial) and bilateral moral hazard (plaintiff and defendant may have limited incentives to disclose appropriate information to each other).

j) Economics of civil procedure: Judicial interest rate

In the traditional law and economics, the judicial interest rate seems uninteresting given the efficient design of tort or contract law. Conventional legal scholarship simply applies a rule to calculate present values that reflect the delays of litigation. Yet, judicial interest rates influence the duration and length of legal proceedings.

Take a simple example. Let us assume that plaintiff was harmed, and the value of defendant's wrongdoing was equivalent to 1,000. Suppose there is a 10 percent discount rate. One could be tempted to consider compensation at trial to be 1,100. The traditional approach suggests that a general interest rate, usually statutorily set, can appropriately meet that result, being at the same time neutral and easy to be implemented.

This simple approach is flawed. When opportunity costs are asymmetric (which is likely), a judicial interest rate will influence delays (beyond social optimality) and decoupling (damages paid by defendant and recovery collected by plaintiff), which shapes the effect of deterrence as well as the process of litigation. An efficient judicial interest rate must consider all these factors and results. Because it would be unrealistic for all these conditions to be satisfied within a single mechanism for determining the judicial interest rate, one must consider and discuss the advantages and disadvantages of applying the second-best solutions.

Furthermore, there are many alternative mechanisms for determining delays and decoupling. If these mechanisms were adequately applied, a judicial interest rate would be trivial and unimportant. However, because these mechanisms have significant limitations of their own when applied in practice, a judicial interest rate plays an important role. It could be that judicial interest rates are more important in civil-law jurisdictions where rules of procedure are perceived to be less flexible.

Asymmetric distribution of opportunity costs is a major source of complexity in this context. Inevitably, the best way to determine a judicial interest rate that internalizes these effects involves leaving the decision-making authority to the parties, as they have better information about their own opportunity costs. However, in much the same way settlements fail, parties to a case may be unable to agree on a judicial interest rate (due to significant transaction costs). The next best approach could be for a court to determine the judicial interest rate. The benefits of a judge's access to information about the parties and his to the case seem to outweigh the possible costs of uncertainty, court error, and additional litigation costs. Still, statutory approaches appear to be more adequate for postjudgment interest when it is clear that the defendant merely seeks to postpone a legal obligation established by judgment.

Court-imposed and statutory judicial interest rates raise different considerations. In theory, it seems that the ability to consider individual preferences and localized information could surpass administrative and litigation costs. Hence, a court-imposed interest rate might be more appropriate in many circumstances. However, at the end of the day, this is a matter of empirical debate and, unfortunately, there is no such quantitative work easily available today.

Many jurisdictions struggle with excessive delays in litigation and consider variations on judicial interest rates as mechanisms for deterring congestion. The effects might be complex and possibly counterproductive. Increasing judicial interest rates to punish noncompliant defendants may result in frivolous delays sponsored by the plaintiff. Decreasing judicial interest rates to sanction noncompliant plaintiffs could induce frivolous delays as well, but the defendant would instead support this result. If judicial interest rates are used to set appropriate delays, they might still cause excessive decoupling or reverse decoupling, which in turn may result in too many or too few lawsuits. Finding an appropriate balance between all these effects and outcomes is not easy when applied in practice. Unfortunately, reform of judicial interest rates may, in many circumstances, result in aggravating, rather than alleviating, court congestion.

From a comparative law perspective, changing judicial interest rates should be considered in the context of alternative procedural reforms. The determination of compensatory and punitive damages could presumably be designed to punish frivolous litigation strategies or determine the number of lawsuits to be filed. Court fees may be structured to achieve decoupling without a need for adjusting the interest rate: both parties pay court fees to the court instead of to each other, therefore explicitly and directly effectuating the targeted decoupling effect. Procedural rules that allow the court to punish either party for purely strategic delays, while circumventing the complications of balancing opportunity costs, are likely to be more appropriate.

The institutional context and design are important when considering how to reform the mechanisms for determining the judicial interest rate. Although the judicial interest rate makes up part of procedural mechanisms that have relevant effects on litigation, the strategies on which its manipulation is based may not produce the expected result or desirable consequence.

It is not being suggested that the judicial interest rate is irrelevant, should not play a role, or cannot be used for purposes of legal reform. The point is much more nuanced than that—judicial interest rate interacts with other available procedural mechanisms. In some cases, it is important to correct the judicial interest rate in order to improve litigation. In other cases, if the judicial interest rate is used to shape litigation and delays, then it is not the most efficient policy instrument, as identical or similar results could be achieved by other legal reforms at a lower cost. Finally, one recognizes that there are many cases where the manipulation of the judicial interest rate would be a poor economic decision because its intended incentives would be incorrectly influenced. A similar reasoning needs to be applied in the context of deciding between court-based and statutory mechanisms to set the judicial interest rate. Here, however, it may be important to distinguish between prejudgment and postjudgment interest.

Prejudgment interest should reflect the appropriate incentives for inducing efficient behavior in litigation. It is likely that the court is in a better position than the legislature to assess the opportunity costs of the parties to a case. Furthermore, with a case-specific inquiry, the judicial interest rate can be enforced as part of the substantial judgment. The interest rate may also easily reflect strategic and frivolous delays made by either party. However, there are uncertainty costs that are borne by potential litigants under the case-by-case method, which is minimized by a statutory determination of the judicial interest rate. It seems that, in the most reasonable circumstances, the benefit of setting an interest rate with more knowledge about the parties offsets the costs of uncertainty.

A different reasoning might apply to postjudgment interest, where the court is concerned with delay in payment. At this stage in the litigation process, the plaintiff's damage is already adjudged. A statutory mechanism for setting the judicial interest rate seems to avoid further costly court intervention more adequately. The cost of administration is lower and there are advantages with respect to information, such as reducing uncertainty and clarifying the immediate costs of delaying payment.

The role of the judicial interest rate seems a trivial question in economic reasoning but is actually highly complex. Its legal policy implications are significant. Furthermore, depending on the institutional context, available procedural approaches and legal family (common or civil-law jurisdiction), the judicial interest rate applied may deserve to be treated differently.

k) Comparative business law and economics: Brief overview

Comparative corporate law and economics has probably attracted the most attention from legal economists. There is extensive literature on the economic reasoning and consequences of the different legal frameworks regulating how companies are formed, investors operate and managers make decisions. The way legal systems have tackled the separation of control and ownership varies considerably, and it has been at the heart of the debate. In particular, the advantages and disadvantages of the Anglo-American market-based system (disseminated ownership) versus the long-term large investor model of Germany (concentrated ownership) have been widely debated. Economic reasoning for limited liability of stockholders, the different role of bondholders (debt versus equity) and the rules of corporate governance addressing agency costs are standard topics in this discussion. Another area that has been addressed is the significant differences in the legal treatment of trusts.

Recent literature has developed a new field called "law and finance" that investigates the extent to which corporate performance, ownership, and organization are influenced by potential legal determinants or what forms of law enforcement provide a more successful regulation of the market for securities.

The sharp contrast between corporate and personal bankruptcy law in the United States has raised questions concerning the economic adequacy of each model. Legal economists analyzed corporate reorganization, liquidation and a fresh start in the American tradition and the extent to which employment goals should prevail in bankruptcy in the French tradition. At the same time, the differential use of bankruptcy law and its effects on credit markets, contractual performance and business environment have deserved attention. Finally, the identification of successful procedural and substantive rules of bankruptcy has been related to the broader issue of legal origin.

Alongside corporate and bankruptcy law, antitrust law and economics is the field that more rapidly has been under the scrutiny of law and economics. It includes the neoclassical analysis of monopolies and oligopoly models as well as natural monopoly and price regulation. Specific substantive issues (concerning cartel behavior, unilateral conduct and mergers and acquisitions) and procedural approaches (judicial versus administrative enforcement of competition law) have been at the heart of economic analysis. For example, optimal fines, per se rule versus the rule of reason, market contestability and the treatment of intellectual property (patents create a monopoly) have generated an extensive economic literature.

Chapter 6

COMPARATIVE ADMINISTRATIVE LAW AND ECONOMICS[1]

Comparative administrative law studies the role of administrative law in different legal systems across the world and possibly at the global level. Law and economics brings the economic perspective to such an analysis. The purpose of comparative administrative law and economics is, in the first place, to provide a rational choice theory to explain why features of administrative law vary across jurisdictions. A second goal is to relate these varying features of administrative law to economic performance (as measured by macroeconomic variables or more specific variables such as rule of law, judicial effectiveness, governance indicators or quality of legal institutions). Finally, there is a normative dimension related to the inevitable question of which arrangements or institutions produce better results.

Economic theory has an enormous literature on regulation. At its core, one finds the principal–agent model explaining procurement and regulatory action. In its simplest formulation, the model clarifies the relationship between a principal (the actor with less information) and an agent (the actor with more information). The conflict of interest between the principal and the agent is embodied by agency costs (a standard form of transaction costs, that is, a net loss due to individual opportunism). These costs exist because the agent might use her information advantage to expropriate the principal from his gains, prompting the principal to design mechanisms to limit such opportunism by the agent. Ideally, the principal can find mechanisms (contractual or otherwise) to align the interests of the agent with his own goals.

There are multiple versions of the principal–agent model. Depending on the nature of the principal and/or the agent, principal–agent models are known in literature under different labels, from political economy to public choice theories. Not surprisingly, the application of the numerous insights from this vast literature to administrative law is immediate.

---

1 Extensive parts of this chapter follow from Garoupa and Amaral-Garcia (2021).

a) Models of administrative adjudication

In a modern economy, there are many disputes between private parties and state agencies. Every country must have a complex system to address such disputes. A quick look around the world shows a variety of ways to address administrative adjudication. In his important article, Asimow (2015) considers five models of administrative adjudication. For example, France and Germany are presented as broadly similar models. Common-law countries are separated between the United States (with combined function agencies) and the British and commonwealth world (with administrative tribunals). The European Union is a different model due to a combination of two features: absence of specialized courts (the nature of the European Court of Justice could be a matter of debate in this regard) and closed judicial review.

These five models respond to balancing three goals within a certain institutional context: accuracy (achieving the correct result), efficiency (avoiding delays and minimizing private and public costs) and fairness (making administrative adjudication acceptable). Therefore, there is no practical reason to suppose that one model is normatively better than another. All the models seek to find the appropriate balance of accuracy, efficiency and fairness. No system is intrinsically superior. At the same time, all five models can be improved if a transplant is carefully designed and strategically implemented.

The five models result from some historical path dependence and a combination of legal culture and political compromise. Inevitably, there are possible rational choice theory explanations to make sense of why certain institutional features produce different models. One is the political system. Under this theory, in a parliamentary regime and unified government, agencies cannot really deviate significantly from the wishes of the political executive branch (since a parliamentary majority can always amend the law ex post). In a presidential system, agencies can be more innovative and diverge from the executive branch. Therefore, while judicial review can be an effective check against actions by the agency in a presidential regime, there is much less demand in a parliamentary regime. This reasoning is critical to explain differences between U.S. and European jurisdictions.

A second theory looks to the political economy analysis of administrative adjudication to explain the observed variations in comparative administrative law. In particular, the economic model expands to consider additional features: delegation to agencies, exercise of discretion by agencies and the role of administrative review. The political regime (presidential versus parliamentary) and the structure of government (unified versus federal) are important institutional factors. They are labeled government concentration in the economic model. Government concentration might contextualize why agencies have low or high autonomy. Concentrated government favors low autonomy whereas dispersed government leans toward high autonomy. However, there is a second dimension—legal institutions that shape the interaction between agencies and the executive branch. In this case, one faces the traditional distinction between characteristics usually associated with the common-law system (recognition judiciary and general courts) and the civil-law system (career judiciary and specialized courts). The economic scholarship suggests that making a distinction between low and high autonomy of courts addresses differences in judicial culture.

The interaction of these two dimensions—political and legal—creates varying realities where certain features of administrative adjudication emerge as rational choice strategies. Different patterns of regulatory behavior and court deference emerge as rational responses to identical problems conditioned on exogenous parameters. Once the arrangements concerning administrative adjudication are perceived as rational responses to a bundle of institutional factors, the literature provides testable hypotheses by combining the classical common-law/civil-law distinction (court autonomy) with political realities (agency autonomy).

A third theory adds a new dimension—the availability of nonjudicial mechanisms to address divergences between the executive branch and agencies, including watchdogs and other safeguard procedures. The insight is that the choice between courts and nonjudicial agents depends on a set of embedded features: transaction costs from overruling judicial decisions, available information to the different actors and political turnover.

b) Specialized agencies

Regulatory agencies are powerful institutions. Influenced by the institutional design developed in the United States in the early part of the twentieth century, they have expanded to Europe and beyond. The agencies combine investigation and prosecution. To some extent, they also play important roles in rulemaking and adjudication. This seems to be a feature of administrative adjudication in the United States and in civil-law jurisdictions. The UK has been a clear outlier for a long time but continues to push the process of integration further. This is embodied by the controversial Regulatory Enforcement and Sanctions Act 2008. An economic framework to explain the advantages and disadvantages of combined function specialized agencies has been considered in the economic literature. There are various benefits of integration: reduction of transaction costs (facilitating coordination in enforcing administrative law), specialization (allowing better use of knowledge and human capital in shaping administrative law), fast track intervention (developing better procedures and concentrating resources on potentially more beneficial regulatory policies) and "monopoly power" (fewer bodies involved in settling disputes reinforce the ability of administrative law enforcement). In addressing the disadvantages, one should include multiple error costs. Depending on their nature, these errors can be of three types: (1) informational (lack of monitoring and auditing), (2) behavioral (due to prevalent biases in administrative decision making) or (3) simply due to capture (by external private interests). Particularly associated with the possibility of capture is the lack of accountability to external institutions.

The balance of costs and benefits explains differences across law—criminal law versus administrative law, but also across jurisdictions. Integrated or combined function agencies may respond to specific concerns. Legal traditions and political processes may contextualize different institutional design. However, the economic theory of integration suggests an alternative model to explain why combined function agencies might be more prevalent in certain jurisdictions than others. Specifically, the reduction of transaction costs, on one side, and the multiplication of error costs, on the other side, could highlight why all jurisdictions do not adjust to the same model. Since these dimensions differ across jurisdictions, so do institutional choices.

c) Specialized courts

Courts play an obvious crucial role in adjudicating administrative cases, and their decisions have an impact on citizens and society. Considering the role that courts play, it is important to understand whether cases involving the government should be adjudicated by specialized administrative courts. The discussion on specialized courts is a contentious one, with several arguments being presented against and in favor of courts' specialization. Overall, the broad implications of having specialized courts in general, and administrative courts in particular, should be assessed taking into account the costs and benefits of specialization. At the same time, it is highly possible that these costs and benefits vary across jurisdictions.

There are several benefits of specialization. Specialized courts can bring out the "neutral virtues" of specialization. In the judiciary, these "neutral virtues" are the quality of decisions, uniformity of the law and efficiency. When judges become experts in certain types of decisions, in principle, more correct decisions in complex areas of the law might arise. This could be particularly relevant in fields of law that require complex technical skills. Specialization might also result in court decisions that are more uniform and coherent. As it is recognized in behavioral law and economics, experts are more likely to overcome certain cognitive biases, such as availability and representativeness, due to their knowledge and experience. One potential advantage of specialized administrative courts is that judges acquire appropriate training so that they become experts in administrative law, and procedures in court can be tailored to deal with the particular features of the government as defendant. When courts are specialists in administrative law, it is possible to develop a set of principles that recognize the distinctiveness of the control of the administration, and procedures can be simpler than those used in private litigation. Judges specialized in administrative law might be more confident when deciding administrative cases given their expertise and specific legal knowledge. As a result, they might be better prepared and more willing to go against administrative decisions.

There are potential disadvantages to specialization as well. Generally speaking, experts are more vulnerable to certain types of biases such as overconfidence and confirmation bias. When it comes to courts, specialization in a particular field of law might result in a narrower application of the law. Moreover, specialized adjudicators might have fewer skills in applying concepts from other areas of law when necessary. A potential loss of the generalist perspective is considered one of the most negative effects of courts' specialization. It is also worth mentioning that the discussion on specialized courts should consider the legal structure as a whole. For example, if first instance courts are specialized but appeals are decided by a general court, there might be some additional issues to consider. Appeals from a specialized court to a generalized court might have higher reversal rates, or damages might be adjusted more frequently if some specificities or peculiarities are not fully understood.

There are potentially significant disadvantages of specialized administrative courts in particular. Specialization in administrative law makes accountability more difficult because the knowledge of administrative law becomes a specific asset on human capital for administrative judges. As in many other contexts, specialization concentrates knowledge, therefore making accountability and transparency more difficult. In this context, judges become more dependent on (or more easily constrained by) the government and bureaucrats precisely because there are fewer sources of legal knowledge. The marginal cost for judges in deciding against the state or the government could be higher in administrative courts than in ordinary judicial courts. If so, capture by the government is more likely in administrative than in civil courts. In this case, capture might result from hindsight bias: administrative courts may have difficulty understanding that the government might have overreached in relation to the appropriateness of intervention. This can arise either because of a cognitive bias (e.g., the existence of the state is not to be questioned) or, more simply, because of self-preservation as state officials.

These biases might result in administrative courts favoring the government, which is undesirable. Courts should not have a bias in favor of any particular party in the litigation process, and the same considerations apply when the government is involved. This is particularly relevant considering that the government is a constant presence in many spheres of daily life, its powers vast and its functions quite complex, and that the government has specific functions that private citizens do not have. Whether the government fares better than private parties in the litigation process is an empirical question—and a difficult one to answer, given the difficulty in finding similar cases that only differ with respect to the type of litigants. There is some evidence that the government can fare better than private parties in terms of different outcomes such as case duration or in obtaining reviews or reversals.

Government favoritism raises concerns, especially during an expansion of the courts' role in determining public policy outcomes (judicialization). All in all, society has a vested interest in ensuring citizens are not treated disadvantageously when dealing with the government; otherwise, they might refrain from bringing their claims forward against a more powerful party.

In civil-law tradition countries, it is common to find a division of jurisdictions with separate sets of courts. Civil-law tradition countries make a strong distinction between private and public law, and administrative courts specialize in administrative law. Despite this common feature in civil-law tradition countries, there is no unique model for administrative courts or for the adjudication of litigation involving the government. Still, the separation of jurisdictions has been considered as an example of inefficiency in legal governance in civil-law tradition countries as argued by the legal origins' theory.

d) State liability: Torts, contracts and procedure

The law that governs state liability in torts and in contracts has attracted attention by legal economists. An initial wave of articles attempted to provide efficiency explanations for why the government should get special treatment, that is, why tort and contract rules applicable to the government might be distinct from those applicable to private parties. Mostly, the reasons are related to the principal–agent problem within the structure of the state. Three possible situations are relevant—when decisions affect different government bodies, when decisions require interaction of different layers of public administration and when decisions are made by governments subject to change (hence the initial action is by an incumbent government and liability is borne by a new government). Remedies that are possibly efficient for private actors could enhance wrongdoings or contractual breach due to the process of allocating authority for decisions within the government.

A second wave of articles addresses more directly comparative aspects. State liability has three goals in any given jurisdiction—provide incentives for government and private actors to act efficiently, remove incentives for private actors when incentives are distorted due to the principal–agent problem within the government and generate information about inefficient behavior by public bodies and agencies to higher levels of government or to the public in general. These goals can be contradictory and respond to varying costs and benefits.

There are sound economic explanations for why state liability regimes may differ across jurisdictions. Certain determinants, such as a preference for strong state intervention in the economy or in society, extensive public employment or weak independent regulatory agencies, could justify different institutional arrangements. To the extent that the solution to a principal–agent model relies on the preferences of the principal and these preferences are ideological in nature, unless one suspects all jurisdictions are politically similar, it is only natural that one finds different legal solutions to tort and contract state liability.

Variation is consistent with an economic explanation based on efficiency, but variation itself is not evidence of efficiency. Whereas the literature on contracts seems to point out that, in general, the common-law principles of state liability are consistent with efficiency, no overall conclusion currently exists for civil-law principles. As for torts, the literature is even less conclusive concerning both legal families.

Governments also benefit from certain procedural advantages in litigation. These procedural advantages might reduce the incentive to litigate against the government, but they also impact the settlement ranges in ways that could complicate settlements and litigation. Yet, extreme rules such as prohibiting out of court settlements in administrative litigation could find economic rationale when agency costs are very significant within the government. There is, however, a lack of empirical comparative literature to highlight general conclusions.

Chapter 7

COMPARATIVE JUDICIAL POLITICS[1]

Comparative judicial politics is a growing field in the intersection of political science (more specifically, comparative politics), comparative law and law and economics (in particular, concerning rational choice theory models of judicial behavior). Originally dominated by the U.S. theoretical and empirical literature about federal courts (overwhelmingly influenced by the U.S. Supreme Court), it has expanded to many different courts, jurisdictions and experiences.[2]

a) Models of judicial behavior

There are different theories developed to explain judicial decision making. Formalists take the view that judges simply interpret and apply the law in a conformist view. Formal legal sources matter and judges do conform to precedent and legalist interpretations of the law on many occasions. In a completely different perspective, the attitudinal model sees judicial preferences. It poses that ideology is paramount in explaining how judges vote in collegial courts. However, ideology comes into play within a complex set of various interactions between politics, social experiences, public opinion, judicial philosophies, social norms, modes of behavior in the judiciary and many other considerations that vary across jurisdictions. Finally, agency theorists recognize the importance of judicial preferences but argue that they are implemented considering political and institutional realities.

Whatever model prevails, judicial behavior in any court is the result of personal attributes, attitudes (including policy or ideological preferences), peer pressure, intracourt interaction (a natural pressure for consensus and court reputation; a common objective to achieve supremacy of judicial branch)

---

1 Extensive parts of this chapter follow Escresa and Garoupa (2013), Garoupa (2011) and Garoupa and Grajzl (2020).
2 See Volcansek (2019) for an introduction to comparative judicial politics.

and party politics (loyalty to the appointer) within a given legal and doctrinal environment.

For example, constitutional judges are appointed by heavily politicized bodies and could be heavily influenced by political parties when these play an active role in the appointment process. Therefore, judicial independence becomes an issue. However, judges are also somehow interested in maintaining a certain status quo that does not hurt the prestige of the court, thereby, keeping some distance from active party politics. In fact, conformity between constitutional judges and party interests can be explained by two different phenomena. First, given the political choice of constitutional judges, they exhibit the same preferences as the party that selects them (i.e., there is an ideological congruence). Second, when the constitutional judges do not have lifetime appointments, they might want to keep a good relationship with the party that selected them for future appointments to the court or elsewhere (regardless of whether the terms are renewable or not). In both models, judges have a politically biased incentive and are not fully independent, but the underlying reasons are significantly different.

As one knows, the process of recruitment and the appointment of judges are necessarily major variables in the design of courts. Overly party-oriented mechanisms are especially bad for independent judicial review but are quite likely to smooth conflicts with other political bodies of government. Cooperative mechanisms that require a supermajority deliver consensual courts, which are more deliberative than active lawmakers.

b) Dissent theory

Disagreement in collegial courts is inevitable. The question of why judges decide to issue separate opinions (concurring or dissenting) in some circumstances but not others has attracted considerable attention, including within comparative legal scholarship. To explain variation in the formation and frequency of separate opinions in distinct jurisdictions, observers typically resort to explanations emphasizing differences in legal traditions. According to the prevailing view, cross-jurisdictional differences in the frequency of separate opinions arise because some legal traditions are inherently more inclined than others to promote judicial dissent.

There are two distinct, but not mutually exclusive, debates under the label "dissent theory." The normative debate focuses on the advantages and disadvantages of separate opinions in collegial courts. Arguments supporting the existence of separate opinions are rooted in beliefs about the benefits of free speech, democratic values and judicial independence, the moral obligation a judge has vis-à-vis the law when her interpretation differs from the court majority, improved case law because of better argued majority opinions, and evolutionary gains within a dialogue between past and future courts. Arguments opposing separate opinions invoke expected negative effects that dissents and concurrences may have on public confidence in the court and court legitimacy, legal certainty, judicial independence, the role of international courts and collegiality, the efficient use of court resources and compliance with court decisions.

The positive debate revolves around a related, but distinct, question: given the possibility of separate opinions, what explains a judge's decision to break with the majority opinion? When judges have the option to concur or dissent, that is, write a separate opinion, they face a multiplicity of considerations. Moreover, a judge may disagree, partially or fully, with the majority opinion and yet decide not to file a formal separate opinion. At the same time, a norm of consensus promotes collegiality.

One must distinguish three sets of theories explaining the incidence of separating opinions: individual rational choice theories, principal–agent accounts and explanations based on legal tradition. According to individual rational choice dissent theory, a potential dissenter balances the costs and benefits of issuing a dissenting opinion (the analysis also applies to concurring opinions, where the magnitude of costs and benefits is likely to be smaller). In doing so, any potential dissenter must recognize that reaching a different outcome than the court majority requires additional costly effort. Furthermore, dissenting has an external cost: it demands additional effort from the majority to answer the dissenter's arguments (either in terms of revising the original opinion to accommodate the dissenter's viewpoint or in responding to her objections). Repeated, forceful and extensive dissents are likely to make it more difficult for the dissenter to gain support from her peers in future cases and may even affect job satisfaction, generating a significant collegiality cost. Dissents may thereby harm the legitimacy of the court and even diminish the probability of compliance with its decisions, two consequences that judges are likely to care about.

Potential dissenters must weigh these important costs against the expected benefits of putting forth a dissenting opinion. Benefits from dissent include the possibility to develop a reputation and express a viewpoint, which results in personal satisfaction as well as the chance to influence case law and policy. Based on the cost–benefit analysis, a judge may ultimately forgo the opportunity to formally dissent even if her ideological preference is different from the one expressed by the majority.

Another group of theories views separate opinions as reflecting principal–agent dynamics. Within a principal–agent model, where judges are agents (with more information about the law) and politicians or upper courts are the principals (with less information about the law), separate opinions are a mechanism through which the agents can align their interests with those of their principals. Dissents therefore facilitate signaling. For example, a dissent allows a lower-court judge to convey information to likeminded, higher-court judges about a particular legal question that requires implementation of additional case law or a change in precedent. Alternatively, a separate opinion enables a judge to truthfully reveal her preferences to her political or ideological constituency. In either case, by issuing a separate opinion, the dissenting judge obtains future career benefits. In each instance, dissent is a credible signal precisely because it is costly and unlikely to be imitated by judges with differing views. Therefore, a separate opinion is valuable because it discloses information.

The interaction between the information conveyed by a separate opinion and the legitimacy of the court plays an important role. More controversial laws may be associated with more dissent due to the intensity of the political debate that they instigate. Alternatively, more controversial laws might require a more decisive intervention by a court of law, which hinders judicial legitimacy and, in turn, deters potential separate opinions. The principal–agent theory of separate opinions is, therefore, complex.

An empirical application of the principal–agent explanations is found in the ideal-points literature. This empirical scholarship conceptualizes dissents as a mechanism for revelation of judicial preferences and leverages dissents to identify ideology-based behavioral clusters. For example, the traditional conservative–progressive axis used to describe the U.S. Supreme Court is supported by ideal-points estimation. Identified ideal points, in turn, reflect dissents.

A related strand of contributions emphasizing principal–agent factors finds that dissenting opinions are more frequent when judges have strong ideological preferences and when judicial preferences differ significantly over policy outcomes. Frequency of dissent is further related to norms of consensus and the influence of politically motivated appointments. Within the same court, reforms that enhance party participation in judicial selection erode consensus. Finally, dissent tends to be more likely when cases are more controversial (especially regarding separation of powers) and when the largest opposition party is politically more relevant.

Legal systems address the possibility of judicial disagreement in a variety of ways. In the common-law tradition, *seriatim* decisions (where each judge enters her own opinion) tended to prevail. Early in its history, the U.S. Supreme Court replaced the traditional seriatim decision with the current system of a court majority opinion where justices can file separate opinions (concurrences or dissents), a practice that became common in the twentieth century. By contrast, in the French *Cour de Cassation* deliberations are kept secret by law and there are no dissenting opinions. Many other courts have mixed practices where dissents are allowed, but efforts are routinely made to find common ground and achieve consensus. While the practice of producing and publicizing dissents extends across common-law countries, civil-law jurisdictions tended to prohibit dissenting opinions. In Belgium, France and Italy, the act of publishing individual judicial views revealed in secret deliberations is deemed unacceptable and, in fact, constitutes a criminal offense. Moreover, when separating opinions in civil-law systems exist, their goal is to enhance legal debate rather than seek changes in doctrinal interpretations or court practices.

Thus, subject to the caveat of important variations within each legal tradition, separate opinions are largely seen as constitutive elements of the common-law traditions, and much less so a part of civil-law traditions. Empirical evidence suggests that the existence or prohibition of separate opinions in a particular legal system is predicated in a complex web of features characteristic of that system. In this sense, the status of separate opinions merely reflects institutional differences embedded in specific legal traditions. The use of separate opinions, as well as the rise of constitutional abstract review in Europe more generally, is therefore under this group of theories explained by legal tradition, history and culture.

c) Strategic defection theory

The strategic defection theory has been developed to capture contextual and institutional differences in courts outside of the United States.[3] The theory explains judicial behavior in unstable or transitional democracies. The departing point is that, in these jurisdictions, judges are not independent, and they are effectively and seriously constrained by political actors in ways different from the standard strategic model. Strategic defection means judges are willing to challenge the executive precisely because they want to distance themselves from appointers whose (future) power and influence are weakening, thus appealing to a strong incoming administration. Consequently, anti-administration decisions should increase at the end of a political cycle.

The model is based on three conditions (which notably are independent of regime type but more likely to be satisfied in transitions): (1) judges can be removed or hurt by the new government (limited tenure), (2) the legislature is weak and therefore all power is concentrated on the executive (the limited role

---

3 Helmke (2004) developed her theory in the context of Argentina.

of the legislature and lack of effective political plurality increase the chances of sanctions against judges; those sanctions are blocked by the legislature in stable mature democracies) and (3) the most significant threat to judges comes not from the incumbent administration (the appointer) but from the following administration, an effect best described as an intertemporal conflict of interest. The first two conditions (possibility of removal and weak legislature) can be seen as inducing strategic behavior. The last condition (significant threat by new administration) ignites defection.

There are two important implications when these three conditions are combined. First, judges will decide more often against the incumbent administration (the appointer) once it is perceivable that they will lose power. Second, judges will concentrate their strategic defection in those cases that are more relevant for the coming administration. As clarified by political scientists, these two behavioral hypotheses have been observed in transitions from authoritarian to democratic regimes as well as in weak democracies such as Argentina and Mexico.

Chapter 8

LAWYERING[1]

The classical economics view is that that regulation pursues public interest when it corrects for market failures. Information asymmetry is the main market failure that applies to professional legal markets. Specifically, for most clients or consumers, professional legal services are credence goods. The explanation is typically the following: a standard consumer is less informed about the nature and quality of the service and must rely on the expertise of the professional lawyer in order to assess (the so-called agency function) and implement the adequate strategy (known as the service function). Under these conditions, the market for professional legal services will fail to produce the socially optimal quantity and quality of legal services. Some protection for the standard consumer of professional legal services is necessary to guarantee quality and mitigate inefficiencies. This protection of legal consumers frequently takes the form of regulation of the legal profession, that is, the supply side of the professional legal services market.

However, asymmetry of information between the demand and supply sides is not the only market failure that economists see in the market for professional legal services. The overall quality of the legal system is positively related to the quality of lawyers. The consequences of poor representation, for example, go beyond the direct client and generate serious negative externalities to the public. A poorly drafted will, for example, will likely have to be litigated, consuming judicial resources. Regulation is justified because the regulatory body will have more information and expertise at judging quality, thereby reducing the negative externality caused by bad lawyering. The converse is also true—regulation can create positive externalities by improving the quality of the justice system via the lawyers that staff and represent that system.

The nature and regulation of legal services limit competition in the market for professional legal services. Alongside asymmetry of information and negative externality, there is another source of potential deadweight loss—lack

1 Extensive parts of this chapter follow from Garoupa and Markovic (2022).

of perfect competition. In particular, lack of perfect competition is a market failure that is either intrinsic to the market for legal services or a regulation failure, a loss imposed by regulation. This is generally referred to as government failure in the public choice literature.

a) Regulation of lawyering

Regulation of lawyering varies across jurisdictions. Nevertheless, broadly speaking, the case for regulating lawyers from a public interest perspective is primarily based on asymmetric information, externality and the possible lack of appropriate competition due to the nature of legal services. The case for deregulation is based on the capture theory that predicts cartel-like behavior: hence lack of appropriate competition due to excessive regulation. While these theories are opposed to one another, they share certain assumptions about professional regulation.

Regulation could simply mean quality regulation, certification and licensing to address adverse selection and moral hazard. The government could subsidize high-quality lawyers to ensure that they remain in the market even if adverse selection persists. Unfortunately, this does not guarantee that the higher quality service will actually be supplied due to moral hazard on the part of attorneys. Alternatively, penalties could be imposed on low-quality lawyers and entry to the market could be restricted to some adequate standard. These sort of regulations, however, require a regulatory agency that must avoid capture and be able to do what consumers allegedly cannot: assess quality and signal it to potential clients.

More generally, under both certification and licensing, a jurisdiction bestows a document (certificate or license) to an individual who satisfies certain conditions. These conditions may be mandatory education or training, thus addressing adverse selection ex ante and moral hazard ex post. The government and private agencies may certify or license professionals, and impose educational and training requirements.

The difference between licensing and self-regulation is that while rules are issued by public authorities in both scenarios (since the professional body is entrusted with public authority), the state regulates entry and performance in the first case (eventually delegated to a private agency independent from the profession) and by the legal profession in the second case. The consequence is that self-regulation promotes strong professional legal associations whereas licensing does not.

The three standard economic arguments against licensing and for self-regulation are the following: (1) licensing does not solve the problem of asymmetric information because neither the government nor a private agency independent from the legal profession can better assess the quality of the services that legal profession provides than the legal profession itself (though they might have better knowledge than the average consumer); (2) licensing does not generate the incentives for the legal profession to invest in collective reputation that sustains high-quality legal services; and (3) licensing is less flexible, which is problematic in dynamic markets where innovation is important, thus generating costs to be borne by the government rather than by the legal profession itself.

b) Deregulation policies

The argument for deregulation concedes that lawyers have the necessary information to produce quality signals in markets for credence goods but cannot avoid the problem of regulatory capture, thus protecting rents. Specifically, lawyers may not pass their better information and expertise to the clients or consumers, increasing search costs for the consumers since asymmetric information will not be reduced. Control and enforcement of quality standards will be ineffective due to collusion within the profession and with regulators, and fees will be set above marginal productive and with a considerable premium.

There are important and immediate rejoinders to the deregulation argument. First, one can develop safeguards to ensure the legal profession does not operate a cartel by designating various watchdogs. Second, self-regulation lowers information costs and may more than compensate for potential losses due to cartel-like behavior. In fact, potential losses from cartel-like behavior can be easily mitigated if there is more than one professional body in competition with each other, a large heterogeneous profession and adequate legal mechanisms (e.g., efficient disciplinary systems).

Nevertheless, the economic deregulation literature has swayed regulators since the early 2000s in some countries (such as the UK or the European Union) more than in others (such as India or Brazil). It maintained that competition would generate quality signals with adequate liability rules and removal of informational barriers, thus addressing the public interest concerns without risking capture. According to this view, appropriate liability rules can provide an effective substitute for professional self-regulation and avoid the problem of cartelization such that the legal market will be more efficient and better serve the public.

Policymakers in many jurisdictions sought to deregulate liberal professions in the 2000s and 2010s with the explicit goal of promoting more competition and better services after a long period of perceived capture by incumbent professional interests. Unlike other services and industries, the regulation of the legal profession had not been traditionally associated with governmental intervention, but rather with strong and influential professional associations. The situation changed in the 2000s when the theory of private capture largely prevailed over concerns about asymmetric information or negative externality. Moreover, due to persistent capture, the implicit assumption was that one can enhance competition in the market for professional legal services without generating more asymmetric information or negative externalities. To promote greater market liberalization, regulators around the world have focused on entry barriers, fees, organizational structures, advertising and professional standards in varying degrees.

Chapter 9

CONCLUSIONS[1]

Here one would like to rephrase the general argument in favor of using law and economics to investigate comparative law topics (and any other legal topics in the vein of any law and legal institution can be studied under the methodology of law and economics). One perceives the field as offering a set of tools that provide a helpful and productive addition to the more standard and traditional legal toolkit. Many of the concepts in microeconomics have legal applications, including comparative law: transaction costs, cooperative surplus, Pareto efficiency, Kaldor–Hicks efficiency, game theory and strategic considerations and behavioral concepts (such as the availability heuristic, confirmation bias, and overoptimism). The importance of empirical work is growing in the study of comparative law.[2]

The recent examples of comparative constitutional law, comparative corporate law and comparative antitrust law (commonly under the label "global antitrust"), three thriving comparative fields at the moment, highlight the importance of access to massive datasets in order to test the innumerable theories out there.[3] However, although data availability is an important factor to consider, it is not the only relevant dimension in this discussion. Important developments in U.S. scholarship, the growing competition of other legal systems in offering alternative solutions to U.S. traditional concepts (in constitutional law, in corporate law or in antitrust law) and significant (and healthy) disagreements in U.S. legal debates—all these induce U.S. scholars to look for answers elsewhere. It could be that these two factors, data availability and looking for answers elsewhere, in combination, explain why constitutional, corporate and antitrust laws have taken the lead while other fields, such as contracts or property, are being slow to catch the trend.

---

1 Extensive parts of this chapter follow from Garoupa and Ulen (2021).
2 A good summary of the empirical literature applied to comparative law is provided by Spamann (2015).
3 Two excellent references are Bradford et al. (2019) and Chilton and Versteeg (2020).

Law and economics has not impacted all fields of law in the same way. While it is difficult to study corporate, antitrust, tax, contract or tort law in the United States without recognizing the insights from law and economics, it is less so in criminal, immigration or family law. This is not the place to argue, positively or normatively, the consequences of that observation. However, the same observation carries to comparative law and economics. Business-related areas (presumably because scholars recognize the importance of market transactions in these fields), when discussed from a comparative perspective, are more likely to be influenced by law and economics. One can easily understand the importance of the legal origins' theory in this context. Other areas of the law (for which the relevance of market transactions is disputable), when debated from a comparative perspective, are less likely to be influenced by law and economics.

Law and economics, as a field of study, has been slow to influence legal scholarship outside of the United States and Israel. Comparative law has not been at the epicenter, to put it mildly, of legal scholarship in the United States, with notable exceptions. It could be just too early to tell if comparative law and economics has a promising, robust future.

It seems clear that comparative law and economics has generated a vast literature in the last decade both in terms of micro and macroanalysis. However, as with economics itself in the mid-twentieth century, a microeconomic foundation of the macroeconomics of comparative law is still missing. The important empirical literature that points out for significant differences at the macro level between the Anglo-American legal family and the civilian families is in need of a sound micro-based theoretical foundation. On the other hand, the economic analysis of particular legal rules in many areas of the law has been developed to a large extent without recognizing the possible macro implications. Legal economists and comparative law scholars should be in an excellent position to mitigate this gap soon.

One also notes that the civil-law/common-law distinction has been asked to do far too much work in fostering comparative law and economics. There are many other tools from both economics and all the behavioral and social sciences that may prove useful in explaining legal differences.

REFERENCES

Acciarri, H. A. and N. Garoupa. 2013. "On the Judicial Interest Rate: A Comparative Law and Economics Perspective." *Journal of European Tort Law* 4: 34.

Anderson, S. 2018. "Legal Origin and Female HIV." *American Economic Review* 108: 1407.

Asimow, M. 2015. "Five Models of Administrative Adjudication." *American Journal of Comparative Law* 63: 3.

Becker, G. 1968. "Crime and Punishment: An Economic Approach." *Journal of Political Economy* 76: 169.

Bentham, J. 1789. *An Introduction to the Principles of Morals and Legislation.*

Bradford, A., A. Chilton, C. Megaw, and N. Sokol. 2019. "Competition Law Gone Global: Introducing the Comparative Competition Law and Enforcement Datasets." *Journal of Empirical Legal Studies* 16: 411.

Bradford, A., Y.-c. Chang, A. Chilton, and N. Garoupa. 2021. "Do Legal Origins Predict Legal Substance?" *Journal of Law and Economics* 64: 207.

Calabresi, G. 1970. *The Costs of Accidents.* New Haven, CT: Yale University Press.

Caterina, R. 2012. "Comparative Law and Economics." In *Elgar Encyclopedia of Comparative Law*, edited by J. M. Smits. Edward Elgar 161–179.

Chilton, A. and M. Versteeg. 2020. *How Constitutional Rights Matter.* Oxford: Oxford University Press.

Coase, R. 1960. "The Problem of Social Cost." *Journal of Law and Economics* 3: 1.

Cooter, R. and T. S. Ulen. 2016. *Law and Economics* (6th ed.). Boston, MA: Addison-Wesley.

De Geest, G., ed. 2009. *Economics of Comparative Law.* Cheltenham: Edward Elgar Publishing.

De Geest, G. 2020. *American Law: A Comparative Primer.* Cheltenham: Edward Elgar Publishing.

Deakin, S. and K. Pistor, eds. 2012. *Legal Origin Theory.* Cheltenham: Edward Elgar Publishing.

Donohue III, J. J. and S. D. Levitt. 2001. "The Impact of Legalized Abortion on Crime." *Quarterly Journal of Economics* 116: 379.

Eisenberg, T. and G. Ramello, eds. 2016. *Comparative Law and Economics.* Cheltenham: Edward Elgar Publishing.

Escresa, L. and N. Garoupa. 2013. "Testing the Logic of Strategic Defection: The Case of the Philippine Supreme Court, 1986–2010." *Asian Journal of Political Science* 21: 189.

Faust, F. 2019. "Comparative Law and Economic Analysis of Law." In *Oxford Handbook of Comparative Law*, edited by M. Reimann and R. Zimmermann (2nd ed.). Oxford: Oxford University Press 827–849.

Garoupa, N. 2011. "Empirical Legal Studies and Constitutional Courts." *Indian Journal of Constitutional Law* 5: 26.

Garoupa, N. 2018. "Law, Economics, and the Courts." In *Oxford Research Encyclopedia of Economics and Finance*, editor in chief J. H. Hamilton. Oxford: Oxford University Press.

Garoupa, N. and T. Ginsburg. 2012. "Economic Analysis and Comparative Law." In *Cambridge Companion to Comparative Law*, edited by M. Bussani and U. Mattei. Cambridge: Cambridge University Press 57–72.

Garoupa, N. and M. Pargendler. 2014. "A Law and Economics Perspective on Legal Families." *European Journal of Legal Studies* 7: 36.

Garoupa, N., C. Gómez Ligüerre, and L. Melón. 2017. *Legal Origins and the Efficiency Dilemma*. Milton Park: Routledge.

Garoupa, N. and P. Grajzl. 2020. "Spurred by Legal Tradition or Contextual Politics? Lessons about Judicial Dissent from Slovenia and Croatia." *International Review of Law and Economics* 63: article number 105912.

Garoupa, N. and S. Amaral Garcia. 2021. "Comparative Administrative Law and Economics." In *Oxford Handbook of Comparative Administrative Law*, edited by P. Cane, H. C. H. Hoffman, E. C. Ip, and P. L. Lindseth. Oxford: Oxford University Press 217–229.

Garoupa, N., R. D. Gill, and L. B. Tide, eds. 2021. *High Courts in Global Perspective: Evidence, Methodologies, and Findings*. Charlottesville, VA: University of Virginia Press.

Garoupa, N. and T. S. Ulen. 2021. "Comparative Law and Economics: Aspirations and Hard Realities." *American Journal of Comparative Law* 69: 664.

Garoupa, N. and M. Markovic. 2022. "Deregulation and the Lawyers' Cartel." *University of Pennsylvania Journal of International Law* 43: 935.

Helmke, G. 2004 *Courts under Constraints: Judges, Generals, and Presidents in Argentina*. Cambridge: Cambridge University Press.

La Porta, R., F. López-de-Silanes, and Andrei Shleifer. 2008. "The Economic Consequences of Legal Origins." *Journal of Economic Literature* 46: 285.

Lawless, R. M., J. K. Robbennolt, and T. S. Ulen. 2016. *Empirical Methods in Law* (2nd ed.). Philadelphia, PA: Wolters Kluwer.

Mattei, U. 1998. *Comparative Law and Economics*. Ann Arbor, MI: University of Michigan Press.

Michaels, R. 2009. "The Second Wave of Comparative Law and Economics?" *University of Toronto Law Review* 59: 197.

North, D. 1990. *Institutions, Institutional Change, and Economic Performance*. Cambridge: Cambridge University Press.

Ogus, A. 2006, *Costs and Cautionary Tales: Economic Insights for the Law*. London: Hart Publishing.

Parisi, F., ed. 2017. *Oxford Handbook of Law and Economics*. Oxford: Oxford University Press.

Posner, R. 1972. *Economic Analysis of Law* (now 9th ed., 2014). Boston, MA: Little Brown.

Reimann, M. and R. Zimmermann, eds. 2019. *Oxford Handbook of Comparative Law* (2nd ed.). Oxford: Oxford University Press.

Riambau, G., C. Lai, B. L. Zhao, and J. Liu. 2020. "Legal Origins, Religion and Health Outcomes: A Cross-Country Comparison of Organ Donation Laws." *Journal of Institutional Economics* 17: 217.

Shavell, S. 2004. *Foundations of Economic Analysis of Law*. Cambridge, MA: Harvard University Press.

Siems, M. 2018. *Comparative Law* (2nd ed.). Cambridge: Cambridge University Press.

Spamann, H. 2015. "Empirical Comparative Law." *Annual Review of Law and Social Science* 11: 131.

Tullock, G. 1997. *The Case against the Common Law.* Durham, NC: Carolina Academic Press.

Volcansek, M. 2019. *Comparative Judicial Politics.* Lanham, MD: Rowman & Littlefield.

Zamir, E. and D. Teichman. 2018. *Behavioral Law and Economics.* Oxford: Oxford University Press.

Zweigert, K. and H. Kötz. 1969. *Einführung in die Rechtsvergleichung auf dem Gebiete des Privatrechts.* Tübingen: Mohr Siebeck.

Zweigert, K. and H. Kötz. 1987. *An Introduction to Comparative Law,* vol. 2. Oxford: Clarendon Press.

INDEX

Milton Keynes UK
Ingram Content Group UK Ltd.
UKHW010132270224
438425UK00001B/2